CABLES

Mittens, Hats & Scarves

CABLES
Mittens, Hats & Scarves

SIXTH&SPRING BOOKS
NEW YORK

SIXTH&SPRING BOOKS
233 Spring Street
New York, New York 10013

Library of Congress Cataloging-in-Publication Data
Library of Congress Control Number: 2007937708

ISBN-10: 1-933027-39-8
ISBN-13: 978-1-933027-39-5

Manufactured in China

3 5 7 9 10 8 6 4

First Edition, 2008

TABLE OF CONTENTS

INTRODUCTION

Classic, deceptively easy to make, and with unisex appeal, cables are considered by many to embody the essence of knitting. The beautiful twists, turns and sways of a cable can be accomplished using just a few simple techniques, and the mittens, hats and scarves in this book provide the perfect small-scale projects for letting your imagination take flight.

If you're new to the world of cables, let yourself be tempted by the Cabled Cap on page 24: knit in the round, it comes together quickly and elegantly. The Striped Hat on page 78 utilizes self-striping yarn to make a colorful statement that works up in a jiffy. More experienced knitters will love sinking their needles into the intricate Three-Cable Scarf on p. 56 and the Traveling Cable Mittens on page 52.

Cables have a unique ability to bring joy to, and continually challenge, knitters. This book gives you all you will need as you embark on the journey. So pick up those dpns and get ready to **KNIT ON THE GO!**

THE BASICS

The wonderful cables in this book are made using only a few simple techniques. (If you aren't yet familiar with how to cable, follow the simple how-tos in this section.) Even beginners will find many of these projects a breeze—from the Striped Hat on page 78 to the Cabled Cap on page 24. Intermediate knitters will delight in the Bomber Hat on page 84, and even experienced knitters will be up for a challenge with the Three-Cable Scarf on page 56. The abundance of projects—more than 20 in all—will keep your curiosity piqued and your knitting skills sharp!

YARN SELECTION

For an exact reproduction of the projects photographed, use the yarn listed in the "Materials" section of the pattern. We've chosen yarns that are readily available in the U.S. and Canada at the time of printing. The Resources list on pages 94 and 95 provides addresses of yarn distributors. Contact them for the name of a retailer in your area.

YARN SUBSTITUTION

You may wish to substitute yarns. Perhaps you view small-scale projects as a chance to incorporate leftovers from your yarn stash, or the yarn specified may not be available in your area. You'll need to knit to the given gauge to obtain the knitted measurements with a substitute yarn (see "Gauge" on the next page). Be sure to consider how the fiber content of the substitute yarn will affect the comfort and the ease of care of your projects.

To facilitate yarn substitution, this book grade yarn by the standard stitch gauge obtained in stockinette stitch. You'll find a grading number in the "Materials" section of the pattern, immediately following the fiber type of the yarn. Look for a substitute yarn that falls into the same category. The suggested needle size and gauge on the yarn label should be comparable to that on the "Standard Yarn Weight" chart (see page 19).

After you've successfully gauge-swatched a substitute yarn, you'll need to figure out how much of the substitute yarn the project requires. First, find the total length of the original yarn in the pattern (multiply number of balls by yards/meters per ball). Divide this figure by the new yards/meters per ball (listed on the yarn label). Round up to the next whole number.

FOLLOWING CHARTS

Charts are a convenient way to follow cables and other stitch patterns at a glance. *Vogue Knitting* stitch charts utilize the universal knitting language of "symbolcraft." When knitting back and forth in rows, read charts from right to left on right-side (RS) rows and from left to right on wrong-side (WS) rows, repeating any stitch and row repeats as directed in the pattern. When knitting in the round, read charts from right to left on every round. Posting a self-

GAUGE

It is always important to knit a gauge swatch, and it is even more so with garments to ensure proper fit.

Patterns usually state gauge over a 4"/10cm span; however, it's beneficial to make a larger test swatch. This gives a more precise stitch gauge, a better idea of the appearance and drape of the knitted fabric, and a chance for you to familiarize yourself with the stitch pattern.

The type of needles used—straight or double-pointed, wood or metal—will influence gauge, so knit your swatch with the needles you plan to use for the project. Measure gauge as illustrated. Try different needle sizes until your sample measures the required number of stitches and rows. *To get fewer stitches to the inch/cm, use larger needles; to get more stitches to the inch/cm, use smaller needles.*

Knitting in the round may tighten the gauge, so if you measured the gauge on a flat swatch, take another gauge reading after you begin knitting. When the piece measures at least 2"/5cm, lay it flat and measure over the stitches in the center of the piece, as the side stitches may be distorted.

It's a good idea to keep your gauge swatch in order to test blocking and cleaning methods.

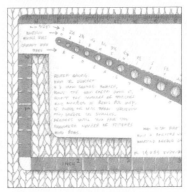

adhesive note under your working row is an easy way to keep track of your place on a chart.

COLORWORK KNITTING

Stranding

The Bias Cable Hat on page 48 uses the stranding method of colorwork. When motifs are closely placed, colorwork is accomplished by stranding two or more colors per row, creating "floats" on the wrong side of the fabric. This technique is sometimes called Fair Isle knitting, after the traditional Fair Isle patterns that are composed of small motifs with frequent color changes.

To keep an even tension and prevent holes while knitting, pick up yarns alternately over and under one another across or around. While knitting, stretch the stitches on the needle slightly wider than the length of the float at the back to keep work from puckering.

Stripes

Many of the projects in this book include stripes. Stripes can be worked with separate balls of each color. These strands are carried along the side of work when not in use. Be sure to keep an even tension of yarn not in use to prevent pulling.

BLOCKING

Blocking is a crucial finishing step in the knitting process. It is the best way to shape pattern pieces and smooth knitted edges in preparation for sewing together. If your project includes specific blocking or pressing instructions, be sure to follow them for best results. Most garments retain their shape if the blocking stages in the instructions are followed carefully. Choose a blocking method according to the instructions on the yarn care label, and when in doubt, test-block your gauge swatch.

Wet Block Method

Using rustproof pins, pin pieces to measurements on a flat surface and lightly dampen using a spray bottle. Allow to dry before removing pins.

Steam Block Method

With wrong sides facing, pin pieces to desired dimensions. Steam lightly, holding the iron 2"/5cm above the knitting. Do not press, or it will flatten stitches.

FINISHING

The pieces in this book use a variety of finishing techniques, from crocheting around the edges to embroidery. Refer to the illustrations for these and other helpful techniques.

SIZING

Unless otherwise stated, all garment patterns are written for an average-size woman.

CARE

Refer to the yarn label for the recommended cleaning method. To clean felted items, wash gently in cool water and take care not to agitate, which will cause the item to felt further.

Stitches picked up along a side edge

1 Insert the knitting needle into the corner stitch of the first row, one stitch in from the side edge. Wrap the yarn around the needle knitwise.

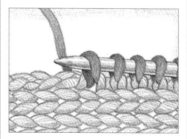

2 Draw the yarn through. You have picked up one stitch. Continue to pick up stitches along the edge. Occasionally skip one row to keep the edge from flaring.

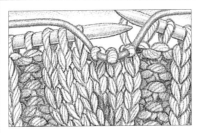

1 Slip the first three stitches of the cable purlwise to a cable needle and hold them to the front of the work. Be careful not to twist the stitches.

1 Slip the first three stitches of the cable purlwise to a cable needle and hold them to the back of the work. Be careful not to twist the stitches.

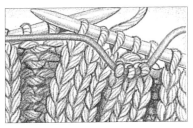

2 Leave the stitches suspended in front of the work, keeping them in the center of the cable needle where they won't slip off. Pull the yarn firmly and knit the next three stitches.

2 Leave the stitches suspended in back of the work, keeping them in the center of the cable needle where they won't slip off. Pull the yarn firmly and knit the next three stitches.

3 Knit the three stitches from the cable needle. If this seems too awkward, return the stitches to the left needle and then knit them.

3 Knit the three stitches from the cable needle. If this seems too awkward, return the stitches to the left needle and then knit them.

There are different ways to make a yarn over. Which method to use depends on where you are in the stitch pattern. If you do not make the yarn over in the right way, you may lose it on the following row, or make a yarn over that is too big. Here are the different variations:

Between two knit stitches: Bring the yarn from the back of the work to the front between the two needles. Knit the next stitch, bringing the yarn to the back over the right-hand needle, as shown.

Between a knit and a purl stitch: Bring the yarn from the back to the front between the two needles. Then bring it to the back over the right-hand needle and back to the front again, as shown. Purl the next stitch.

Between a purl and a knit stitch: Leave the yarn at the front of the work. Knit the next stitch, bringing the yarn to the back over the right-hand needle, as shown.

Between two purl stitches: Leave the yarn at the front of the work. Bring the yarn to the back over the right-hand needle and to the front again, as shown. Purl the next stitch.

Multiple yarn overs (two or more): Wrap the yarn around the needle, as when working a single yarn over, then continue wrapping the yarn around the needle as many times as indicated. Work the next stitch of the left-hand needle. On the following row, work stitches into the extra yarn overs as described in the pattern. The illustration at right depicts a finished yarn over on the purl side.

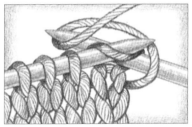

At the beginning of a knit row: Insert the right-hand needle knitwise into the first stitch on the left-hand needle, keeping the yarn in front of the needle. Bring the yarn over the right-hand needle to the back and knit the first stitch, holding the yarn over with your thumb if necessary.

At the beginning of a purl row: Insert the right-hand needle purlwise into the first stitch on the left-hand needle, keeping the yarn behind the needle. Purl the first stitch.

DOUBLE-POINTED NEEDLES

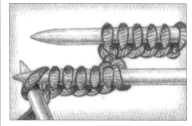

1 Cast on the required number of stitches on the first needle, plus one extra. Slip this extra stitch to the next needle as shown. Continue in this way, casting on the required number of stitches on the last needle.

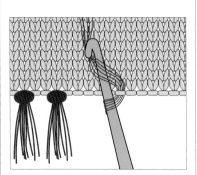

SIMPLE FRINGE: Cut yarn twice desired length plus extra for knotting. On wrong side, insert hook from front to back through piece and over folded yarn. Pull yarn through. Draw ends through and tighten. Trim yarn.

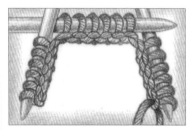

2 Arrange the needles as shown, with the cast-on edge facing the center of the triangle (or square).

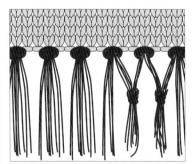

KNOTTED FRINGE: After working a simple fringe (it should be longer to allow for extra knotting), take one half of the strands from each fringe and knot them with half the strands from the neighboring fringe.

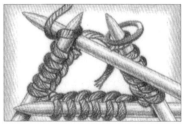

3 Place a stitch marker after the last cast-on stitch. With the free needle, knit the first cast-on stitch, pulling the yarn tightly. Continue knitting in rounds, slipping the marker before beginning each round.

PROVISIONAL CAST-ON

The provisional cast-on, sometimes called open cast-on, is used when you want to have open stitches at the cast-on edge in order to pick up stitches later to work a hem, or if you want to weave these open stitches to the final row of stitches for a smooth seam. There are many different ways to work a provisional cast-on, two of which are described below.

With a Crochet Hook

1 Using waste yarn of a similar weight to the project yarn and a crochet hook appropriate for that yarn, chain the number of cast-on stitches stated in the instructions. Cut a tail and pull the tail through the last chain.

2 Using the needles and working yarn, pick up one stitch through the purl bumps on the back of each crochet chain. Be careful not to split the waste yarn, as this makes it difficult to pull out the crochet chain at the end.

3 Continue working pattern as described.

4 To remove waste chain, pull out the tail from the last crochet stitch. Gently and slowly pull on the tail to unravel the crochet stitches, carefully placing each released knit stitch on a needle.

Long Tail

1 Leaving tails about 4"/10cm long, tie a length of scrap yarn (approximately four times the desired width) together with the main yarn in a knot. With your right hand, hold the knot on top of the needle a short distance from the tip, then place your thumb and index finger between the two yarns and hold the long ends with the other fingers. Hold your hand with your palm facing upward and spread your thumb and index finger apart so that the yarn forms a V with the main yarn over your index finger and the scrap yarn over your thumb.

2 Bring the needle up through the scrap-yarn loop on your thumb from front to back. Place the needle over the main yarn on your index finger and then back through the loop on your thumb. Drop the loop off your

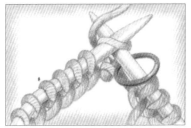

1 Hold the needle tip with the last cast-on stitch in your right hand and the tip with the first cast-on stitch in your left hand. Knit the first cast-on stitch, pulling the yarn tight to avoid a gap.

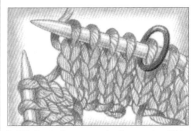

2 Work until you reach the marker. This completes the first round. Slip the marker to the right needle and work the next round.

thumb and, placing your thumb back in the V configuration, tighten up the stitch on the needle.

3 Repeat for the desired number of stitches. The main yarn will form the stitches on the needle and the scrap yarn will make the horizontal ridge at the base of the cast-on row.

4 When picking up the stitches along the cast-on edge, carefully cut and pull out the scrap yarn as you place the exposed loops on the needle.

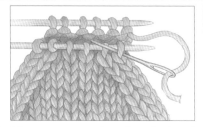

1 Insert tapestry needle purlwise (as shown) through first stitch on front needle. Pull yarn through, leaving that stitch on knitting needle.

2 Insert tapestry needle knitwise (as shown) through first stitch on back needle. Pull yarn through, leaving stitch on knitting needle.

3 Insert tapestry needle knitwise through first stitch on front needle, slip stitch off needle and insert tapestry needle purlwise (as shown) through next stitch on front needle. Pull yarn through, leaving this stitch on needle.

4 Insert tapestry needle purlwise through first stitch on back needle. Slip stitch off needle and insert tapestry needle knitwise (as shown) through next stitch on back needle. Pull yarn through, leaving this stitch on needle.

Repeat steps 3 and 4 until all stitches on both front and back needles have been grafted. Fasten off and weave in end.

Categories of yarn, gauge ranges, and recommended needle and hook sizes

Yarn Weight Symbol & Category Names	**1** Super Fine	**2** Fine	**3** Light	**4** Medium	**5** Bulky	**6** Super Bulky
Type of Yarns in Category	Sock, Fingering, Baby	Sport, Baby	DK, Light Worsted	Worsted, Afghan, Aran	Chunky, Craft, Rug	Bulky, Roving
Knit Gauge Range* in Stockinette Stitch to 4 Inches	27–32 sts	23–26 sts	21–24 sts	16–20 sts	12–15 sts	6–11 sts
Recommended Needle in Metric Size Range	2.25–3.25 mm	3.25–3.75 mm	3.75–4.5 mm	4.5–5.5 mm	5.5–8 mm	8 mm and larger
Recommended Needle U.S. Size Range	1 to 3	3 to 5	5 to 7	7 to 9	9 to 11	11 and larger
Crochet Gauge* Ranges in Single Crochet To 4 Inch	21–32 sts	16–20 sts	12–17 sts	11–14 sts	8–11 sts	5–9 sts
Recommended Hook in Metric Size Range	2.25–3.5 mm	3.5–4.5 mm	4.5–5.5 mm	5.5–6.5 mm	6.5–9 mm	9 mm and larger
Recommended Hook U.S. Size Range	B–1 to E–4	E–4 to 7	7 to I–9	I–9 to K–10½	K–10½ to M–13	M–13 and larger

*Guidelines only: The above reflects the most commonly used needle or hook sizes for specific yarn categories.

SKILL LEVELS FOR KNITTING

■□□□◗
Beginner
Ideal first project.

■■■□◗
Intermediate
For knitters with some experience. More intricate stitches, shaping and finishing.

■■□□◗
Very Easy
Basic stitches, minimal shaping, simple finishing.

■■■■◗
Experienced
For knitters able to work patterns with complicated shaping and finishing.

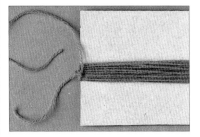

Tassel with shank Wrap yarn around a piece of cardboard that is the desired length of the tassel. Thread a strand of yarn, insert it through the cardboard, and tie it at the top, leaving a long end to wrap around the tassel.

Cut the lower edge to free the wrapped strands. Wrap the long end of the yarn around the upper edge and insert the yarn into the top, as shown. Trim the strands.

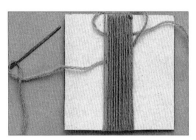

Tassel without shank Wrap yarn around cardboard the length of the tassel, leaving a 12-inch (30cm) strand loose at either end. With a yarn needle, knot both sides to the first loop and run the loose strand under the wrapped strands. Pull tightly and tie at the top.

Cut the lower edge of the tassel and, holding the tassel about three-fourths inch (2cm) from the top, wind the top strands (one clockwise and one counterclockwise) around the tassel. Thread the two strands and insert them through the top of the tassel.

CHAIN

1 Pass the yarn over the hook and catch it with the hook.

2 Draw the yarn through the loop on the hook.

3 Repeat steps 1 and 2 to make a chain.

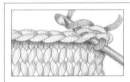

SINGLE CROCHET

1 Insert the hook through top two loops of a stitch. Pass the yarn over the hook and draw up a loop—two loops on hook.

2 Pass the yarn over the hook and draw through both loops on hook.

3 Continue in the same way, inserting the hook into each stitch.

SLIP STITCH

Insert the crochet hook into a stitch, catch the yarn, and pull up a loop. Draw the loop through the loop on the hook.

POMPOMS

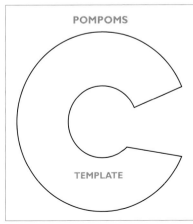

TEMPLATE

1 Following the template, cut two circular pieces of cardboard.

2 Hold the two circles together and wrap the yarn tightly around the cardboard several times. Secure and carefully cut the yarn.

3 Tie a piece of yarn tightly between the two circles. Remove the cardboard and trim the pompom to the desired size.

KNITTING TERMS AND ABBREVIATIONS

approx approximately

beg begin(ning)

bind off used to finish an edge and keep stitches from unraveling. Lift the first stitch over the second, the second over the third, etc. (U.K.: cast off)

cast on a foundation row of stitches placed on the needle in order to begin knitting

CC contrast color

ch chain(s)

cm centimeter(s)

cn cable needle

cont continu(e)(ing)

dc double crochet (U.K.: tr—treble)

dec decrease(ing)—reduce the stitches in a row (knit 2 together)

dpn(s) double-pointed needle(s)

foll follow(s)(ing)

g gram(s)

garter stitch knit every row. Circular knitting Knit one round, then purl one round

hdc half-double crochet (U.K.: htr–half treble)

inc increase(ing)—add stitches in a row (knit into the front and back of a stitch)

k knit

k f & b knit into front and back of stitch

k2tog knit 2 stitches together

k3tog knit 3 stitches together

knitwise (kwise) as if to knit

lp(s) loops(s)

LH left-hand

m meter(s)

M1 make one stitch—with the needle tip, lift the strand between last stitch worked and next stitch on the left-hand needle and knit into the back of it. One stitch has been added

M1 p-st make one purl stitch—work same as M1, but purl instead of knit.

MB make bobble

MC main color

mm millimeter(s)

oz ounce(s)

p purl

p2tog purl 2 stitches together

p3tog purl 2 stitches together

purlwise as if to purl

pat pattern

pick up and knit (purl) knit (or purl) into the loops along an edge

pm place marker—place or attach a loop of contrast yarn or purchased stitch marker as indicated psso pass slip stitch over

rem remain(s)(ing)

rep repeat

rev St st reverse stockinette stitch—purl right-side rows, knit wrong-side rows. Circular knitting: Purl all rounds (U.K.: reverse stocking stitch)

rnd(s) round(s)

RH right-hand

RS right side(s)

sc single crochet (U.K.: dc–double crochet)

S2KP slip 2 sts tog, k1, pass 2 sl sts over k1

sk skip

SKP slip 1, knit 1, pass slip stitch over knit 1

SK2P slip 1, knit 2 together, pass slip stitch over k2tog

sl slip—an unworked stitch made by passing a stitch from the left-hand to the right-hand needle as if to purl

sl st slip stitch (U.K.: single crochet)

ssk slip, slip, knit—slip next 2 stitches knitwise, one at a time, to right-hand needle. Insert tip of left-hand needle into fronts of these stitches from left to right. Knit them together. One stitch has been decreased

st(s) stitch(es)

St st stockinette stitch—knit right-side rows, purl wrong-side rows. Circular knitting: Knit all rounds. (U.K.: stocking stitch)

tbl through back of loop

tog together

tr treble crochet (UK: dtr–double treble)

WS wrong side(s)

w&t wrap and turn

wyif with yarn in front

wyib with yarn in back

work even continue in pattern without increasing or decreasing. (U.K.: work straight)

yd yard(s)

yo yarn over—make a new stitch by wrapping the yarn over the right-hand needle. (U.K.: yfwd, yon, yrn)

* repeat directions following * as many times as indicated

[ ] repeat directions inside brackets as many times as indicated

This sweet cabled cap is sure to become your favorite cold-weather headwear. Designed by Tanis Gray, it features a single rib band and an overall pattern of tiny cables and garter stitch ridges. Easy to knit and great to wear.

KNITTED MEASUREMENTS
■ Head circumference 17"/43cm

MATERIALS
■ 2 1.75oz/50g skeins (each approx 114yd/104m) of Koigu Wool Designs *Kersti* (100% merino wool) in #10104 slate blue
■ Size 6 (4mm) circular needle, 16"/40.5cm long *or size to obtain gauge*
■ One set (5) size 6 (4mm) dpn
■ Cable needle
■ Stitch marker

GAUGE
26 sts and 46 rnds to 4"/10cm over cable pat using size 6 (4mm) circular needle. *Take time to check gauge.*

STITCH GLOSSARY
4-st RC Sl next 2 sts to cn and hold in *back*, k2, k2 from cn.

K1, P1 RIB
(multiple of 2 sts)
Rnd 1 (RS) *K1, p1; rep from * around. Rep this rnd for k1, p1 rib.

CABLE PATTERN
(multiple of 6 sts)
Rnds 1–3 Knit.
Rnd 4 *P2, k4; rep from * around.
Rnd 5 *P2, 4-st RC; rep from * around.
Rnd 6 Knit.
Rep rnds 1–6 for cable pat.

HAT
With circular needle, cast on 102 sts. Join taking care not to twist sts on needle. Place marker for end of rnd and sl marker every rnd. Work in k1, p1 rib for 6 rnds. Cont in cable pat and work until piece measures 7½"/19cm from beg.

Crown shaping
Note Change to dpn (dividing sts evenly between four needles) when there are too few sts on circular needle.
Next rnd *K2tog; rep from * around—51 sts.
Next rnd Knit.
Next rnd K1, *k2tog; rep from * around—26 sts.
Next rnd Knit. Cut yarn leaving a 8"/20.5cm tail and thread through rem sts. Pull tog tightly and secure end.

DOUBLE-CABLE SCARF

Oliver twist

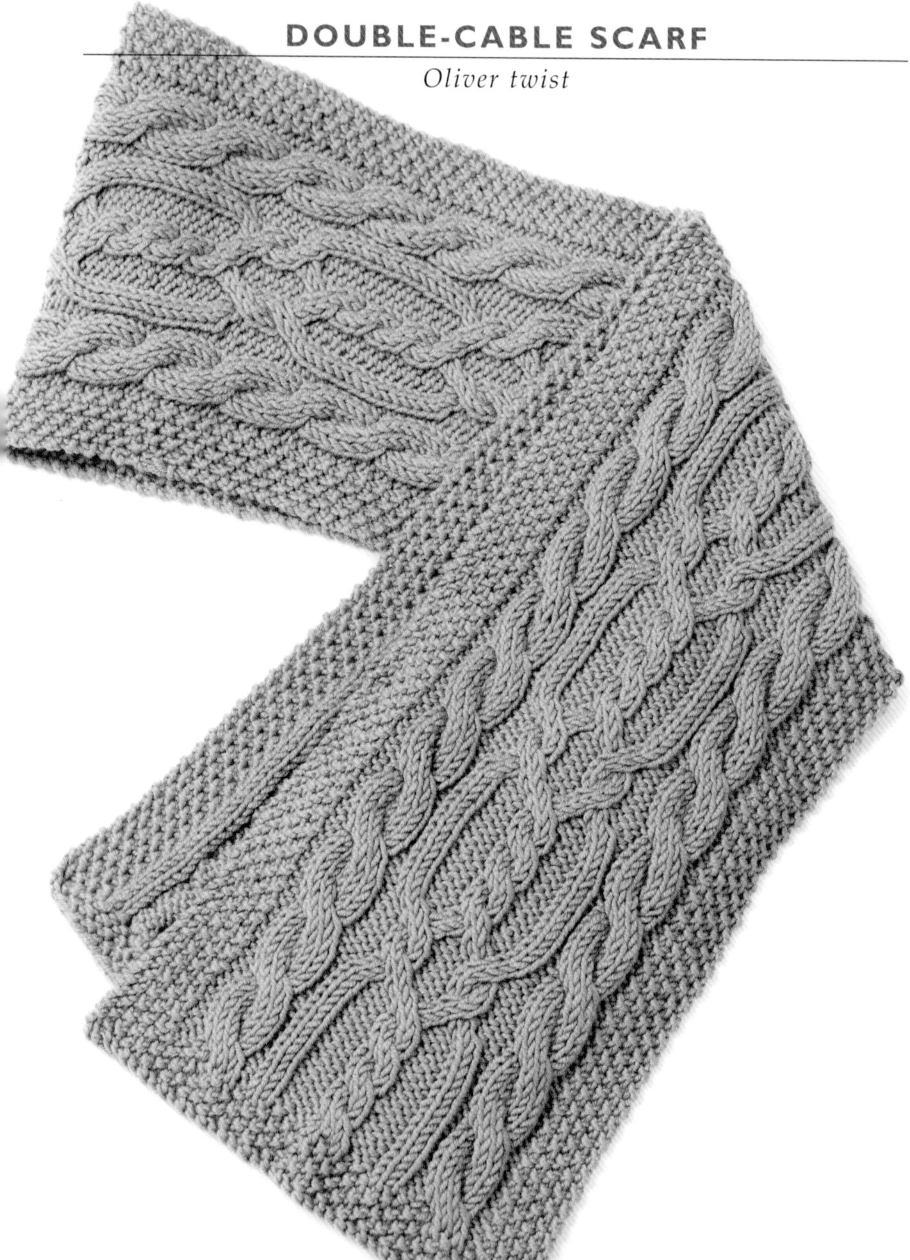

Richly textured cables and luxurious yarn combine to make one elegant scarf. This must-have winter accessory is well worth the effort—it will always be in style. Designed by Monica Jines.

KNITTED MEASUREMENTS
■ Approx 8" x 60"/20.5cm x 152.5cm

MATERIALS
■ 5 1.75oz/50g balls (each approx 94yd/86m) of Sublime/KFI *Cashmere Merino Silk Aran* (75% extrafine merino/20% silk/5% cashmere) in #14 noisette (4)
■ One pair size 8 (5mm) needles *or size to obtain gauge*
■ Cable needle
■ Stitch markers

GAUGE
18 sts and 20 rows to 4"/10cm over Cable pat using size 8 (5mm) needles.
Take time to check gauge.

STITCH GLOSSARY
4-st LPC Sl next 2 sts to cn and hold in *front*, p2, k2 from cn.

4-st RPC Sl next 2 sts to cn and hold in *back*, k2, p2 from cn.

4-st LC Sl next 2 sts to cn and hold in *front*, k2, k2 from cn.

4-st RC Sl next 2 sts to cn and hold in *back*, k2, k2 from cn.

6-st LC Sl next 3 sts to cn and hold in *front*, k3, k3 from cn.

SEED STITCH
Row 1 (RS) K1, *p1, k1; rep from * to end.

Row 2 K the purl sts and p the knit sts. Rep row 2 for seed st.

CABLE PANEL A
(over 10 sts)

Row 1 (RS) P2, 6-st LC, p2.

Rows 2, 4, 6, 8 K2, p6, k2.

Rows 3, 5 and 7 P2, k6, p2.

Rep rows 1–8 for cable panel A.

CABLE PANEL B
(over 16 sts)

Row 1 (RS) K2, p4, 4-st LC, p4, k2.

Row 2 and all WS rows K the knit sts and p the purl sts.

Row 3 K2, p4, k4, p4, k2.

Row 5 Rep row 1.

Row 7 Rep row 3.

Row 9 Rep row 5.

Row 11 4-st LPC, 4-st RPC, 4-st LPC, 4-st RPC.

Row 13 P2, 4-st LC, p4, 4-st RC, p2.

Row 15 P2, k4, p4, k4, p2.

Row 17 Rep row 13.

Row 19 4-st RPC, 4-st LPC, 4-st RPC, 4-st LPC.

Row 21 Rep row 1.

Row 23 Rep row 3.

Row 24 Rep row 2.

Rep rows 1–24 for cable panel B.

SCARF

Cast on 41 sts. Work in seed st for 5 rows.

Set up (inc) row (WS) K1, [p1, k1] twice, k1, M1, p6, k1, M1, p2, k3, M1, p4, k3, M1, p2, k1, M1, p6, k2, k1, [p1, k1] twice—46 sts.

Beg cable pats

Row 1 (RS) Work seed st over first 5 sts, pm, work row 1 of cable pat A, pm, work row 1 of cable pat B, pm, work row 1 of cable pat A, pm, work seed st over last 5 sts.

Row 2 Work seed st over first 5 sts, work row 2 of cable pat A, work row 2 of cable pat B, work row 2 of cable pat A, work seed st over last 5 sts. Cont as established until piece measures 59"/150cm from beg, end on row 7 of cable pat B.

Next (dec) row (WS) Work seed st over first 5 sts, k2tog, p6, k2tog, p2, k2, k2tog, p4, k2, k2tog, p2, k2tog, p6, k2, work seed st over last 5 sts—41 sts. Cont in seed st for 5 rows. Bind off in seed st.

FINISHING

Block lightly to measurements.

Cable Panel A
(10 sts)

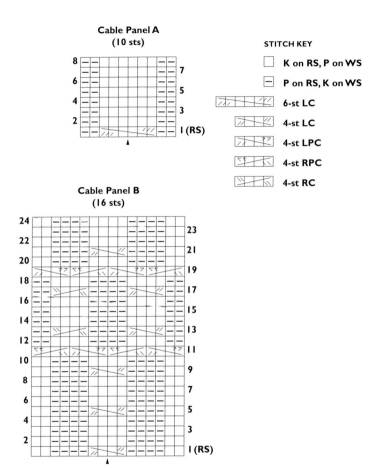

Cable Panel B
(16 sts)

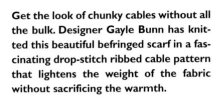

Get the look of chunky cables without all the bulk. Designer Gayle Bunn has knitted this beautiful befringed scarf in a fascinating drop-stitch ribbed cable pattern that lightens the weight of the fabric without sacrificing the warmth.

STITCH GLOSSARY
11-st RC Sl next 6 sts to cn and hold in *back* of work, k2, p1, k2; [p1, k2] twice from cn.
Drop (WS) Drop next st from needle to make a ladder and unravel rows to previous yo below, then work yo to replace dropped st.

SCARF
Cast on 41 sts.
Row 1 (RS) K1, p1, [k2, p1] 3 times, k2, p2, k2, [yo, k2tog, k1] 3 times, p2, [k2, p1] 4 times, k1.

Row 2 K2, *[p2, k1] 3 times, p2, k2; rep from * once more, [p2, k1] 3 times, p2, k2.
Row 3 K1, p1, *[k2, p1] 3 times, k2, p2; rep from * once more, [k2, p1] 4 times, k1.
Row 4 Rep row 2.
Row 5 Rep row 3.
Row 6 Rep row 2.
Row 7 K1, p1, 11-st RC, p2, [k2, p1] 3 times, k2, p2, 11-st RC, p1, k1.
Row 8 Rep row 2.
Row 9 K1, p1, k2, [yo, k2tog, k1] 3 times, p2, [k2, p1] 3 times, k2, p2, k2, [yo, k2tog, k1] 3 times, p1, k1.
Row 10 K2, [p2, k1] 3 times, p2, k2, [p2, Drop] 3 times, p2, k2, [p2, k1] 3 times, p2, k2.
Row 11 K1, p1, [k2, p1] 3 times, k2, p2, 11-st RC, p2, [k2, p1] 4 times, k1.
Rows 12–17 Rep rows 2 and 3 3 times.
Row 18 Rep row 2.
Row 19 Rep row 11.
Row 20 Rep row 2.
Row 21 Rep row 1.
Row 22 K2, [p2, Drop] 3 times, p2, k2, [p2, k1] 3 times, p2, k2, [p2, Drop] 3 times, p2, k2.
Row 23 Rep row 7.
Row 24 Rep row 2.
Row 25 Rep row 3. Rep rows 2–25 until piece measures approx 66"/167.5cm from beg, end on row 4 or 16. Bind off in cable pat.

FRINGE
Cut 14"/35.5cm strands of yarn. Using 4 strands for each, use hook to knot fringe in each purl ditch across each short end. Trim fringe evenly across each end.

Drop-Stitch Cable Pattern
(41 sts)

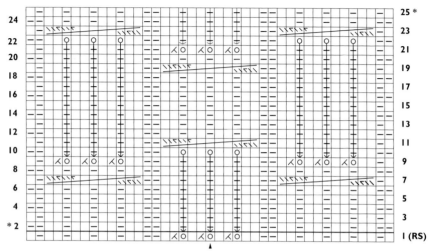

STITCH KEY

☐ K on RS, P on WS

─ P on RS, K on WS

⊡ Yo

⎰ K2tog

⟍⟍⟍⟋⟋ 11-st RC

⊡ Drop

SELF-STRIPING GAUNTLETS

High fives

■ ■ ■ ▭

Function meets fashion: Marla Mutch's trendy gauntlets keep your hands warm while keeping your fingers free. They're worked in the round in an easy cable-knit rib using bright and colorful self-striping yarn.

KNITTED MEASUREMENTS
■ Hand circumference 8"/20.5cm

MATERIALS
■ 3 1.75oz/50g balls (each approx 100yd/91m) of Trendsetter Yarns *Tonalita* (52% wool/48% acrylic) in #2378 country garden ❹

■ One set (4) size 4 (3.5mm) dpn *or size to obtain gauge*

■ Cable needle

■ Stitch holders

■ Stitch markers

GAUGE
24 sts and 28 rnds to 4"/10cm over cable pat using size 4 (3.5mm) dpn.
Take time to check gauge.

K2, P2 RIB
(multiple of 4 sts)
Rnd 1 (RS) *K2, p2; rep from * around.
Rep this rnd for k2, p2 rib.

CABLE PATTERN
(multiple of 8 sts)
Rnds 1–3 (RS) *K4, p4; rep from * around.
Rnd 4 *Sl next 2 sts to cn and hold in *front*,

k2, k2 from cn, p4; rep from * around.
Rnds 5 and 6 Rep rnd 1.
Rep rnds 1–6 for cable pat.

GAUNTLET
Cast on 48 sts dividing sts evenly between 3 dpn. Join taking care not to twist sts on dpn. Place marker for end of rnd and sl marker every rnd. Work in cable pat until piece measures 6"/15cm from beg.

Thumb gusset
Inc rnd 1 Work cable pat across first 4 sts, pm, [M1] twice, pm, work cable pat to end—50 sts. Work next rnd even, working sts between thumb gusset markers in St st.

Inc rnd 2 Work cable pat across first 4 sts, sl marker, M1, k2, M1, sl marker, work cable pat to end—52 sts. Work next rnd even.

Inc rnd 3 Work cable pat across first 4 sts, sl marker, M1, k4, M1, sl marker, work cable pat to end—54 sts. Work next rnd even.

Inc rnd 4 Work cable pat across first 4 sts, sl marker, M1, k6, M1, sl marker, work cable pat to end—56 sts. Work next rnd even.

Inc rnd 5 Work cable pat across first 4 sts, sl marker, M1, k8, M1, sl marker, work cable pat to end—58 sts. Work next rnd even.

Inc rnd 6 Work cable pat across first 4 sts, sl marker, M1, k10, M1, sl marker, work cable pat to end—60 sts. Work next rnd even.

Inc rnd 7 Work cable pat across first 4 sts, sl marker, M1, k12, M1, sl marker, work cable pat to end—62 sts. Work next rnd even.

Inc rnd 8 Work cable pat across first 4 sts, sl marker, M1, k14, M1, sl marker, work cable pat to end—64 sts. Work next 3 rnds even.

Next rnd Work cable pat across first 4 sts, place next 16 sts on two separate holders (8 sts on each) for thumb, work cable pat to end—48 sts. Cont in cable pat until piece measures 12"/30.5cm from beg, end on rnd 6. Bind off in cable pat.

Thumb

Place 16 sts on holders to 3 dpn, dividing sts evenly. Join and place marker for end of rnd and sl marker every rnd. Work in St st for 4 rnds. Cont in k2, p2 rib for 5 rnds. Bind off in rib.

CABLED WRISTLETS AND HAT
Bunny slope

Cecily Glowik has fashioned the sweet-est set from the softest of yarns. The hat and wristlets are worked in stockinette stitch and trimmed beautifully with wide cabled bands that button closed.

Notes
1 Hat cable band and wristlet cable cuffs are worked back and forth in rows.

2 Hat crown is worked in rnds.

3 Wristlets are worked from the bottom up.

STITCH GLOSSARY
6-st LC Sl next 3 sts to cn and hold in *front*, k3, k3 from cn.

CABLE PANEL
(over 29 sts)

Rows 1 and 3 (RS) Sl 1, k3, [p3, k6] twice, p3, k3, sl 1.

Rows 2 and 4 P4, [k3, p6] twice, k3, p4.

Row 5 Sl 1, k3, [p3, 6-st LC] twice, p3, k3, sl 1.

Row 6 Rep row 2.

Rep rows 1–6 for cable panel.

BUTTONHOLE BAND
(multiple of 5 sts plus 2)

Row 1 (RS) K1, yo, *k5, pass the 2nd, 3rd, 4th, then 5th sts over the first st, yo; rep from *, end k1.

Row 2 P1, *work (p1, yo, k1 tbl) in yo, p1; rep from * to end.

Row 3 K2, k1 tbl, *k3, k1 tbl ; rep from *, end k2.

Row 4 Knit.

Work rows 1–4 for buttonhole band.

HAT

Cable band
With straight needles, cast on 29 sts. Work in cable panel until piece measures 21"/53.5cm from beg, end with a WS row. Bind off in cable panel st.

Crown

With RS facing, circular needle and bound-off edge of cable band at RH, pick up and k 84 sts along side edge of cable band. Join and pm for end of rnd and sl marker every rnd. Work around in St st until piece measures 7"/17.5cm from beg (including cable band), end with a WS row.

Crown shaping

Note Change to dpn when there are too few sts on circular needle.

Rnd 1 (RS) *K4, k2tog; rep from * around—70 sts.

Rnd 2 Knit.

Rnd 3 *K3, k2tog; rep from * around—56 sts.

Rnd 4 Knit.

Rnd 5 *K2, k2tog; rep from * around—42 sts.

Rnd 6 Knit.

Rnd 7 *K1, k2tog; rep from * around—28 sts.

Rnd 8 Knit.

Rnd 9 [K2tog] 14 times—14 sts. Cut yarn leaving a 6"/15.5cm tail and thread through rem sts. Pull tog tightly and secure end.

BUTTONHOLE BAND

With straight needles, cast on 22 sts. Work rows 1–4 of buttonhole band. Bind off sts knitwise.

FINISHING

Sew bound-off edge of buttonhole band to bound-off edge of cable band. Lap buttonhole band over cable band and mark placement for 3 buttons on cable band using the 3 center buttonholes as a guide. Sew on ⅝"/16mm buttons.

RIGHT WRISTLET

Cable cuff

With straight needles, cast on 29 sts. Work in cable panel until piece measures 8½"/21.5cm from beg, end with a WS row. Bind off in cable panel st.

Hand

With RS facing, straight needles and cast-on edge of cable cuff at RH, pick up and k 35 sts along side edge of cable cuff. Work in St st until piece measures 4½"/11.5cm from beg (including cable cuff), end with a WS row.

Next (inc) row (RS) K, inc 10 sts evenly spaced across—45 sts. Beg with a p row, cont in St st until piece measures 5½"/14cm from beg (including cable cuff), end with a WS row.

Thumb gusset

Row 1 (RS) K21, pm, k3, pm, k21.

Row 2 P21, sl marker, k3, sl marker, p21.

Row 3 K21, sl marker, M1, k to next marker, M1, sl marker, k21—47 sts.

Row 4 P21, sl marker, k to next marker, sl marker, p21. Rep last 2 rows 7 times more—61 sts (19 garter sts between markers).

Next row (RS) K21, bind off next 19 sts

dropping markers, k to end—42 sts.

Next (joining) row P across all 42 sts closing thumb hole. Cont in St st for 4 rows.

Beg rib pat

Row 1 (RS) K2, *p3, k2; rep from * to end.

Row 2 P2, *k3, p2; rep from * to end. Rep rows 1 and 2 for 1"/2.5cm, end with a WS row. Bind off in rib pat.

Cable cuff

Work as for right wristlet.

Hand

With RS facing, straight needles and bound-off edge of cable cuff at RH, pick up and k 35 sts along side edge of cable cuff. Cont to work as for right wristlet.

With straight needles, cast on 22 sts. Work rows 1–4 of buttonhole band. Bind off sts knitwise.

For each wristlet, sew bound-off edge of buttonhole band to cast-on edge of cable cuff. Lap buttonhole band over cable cuff and mark placement for 3 buttons on cable cuff using the 3 center buttonholes as a guide. Sew on ½"/13mm buttons.

CABLED NECK WARMER

Regency

Get the layered look when you button up in a cozy cabled neck warmer that gives the illusion of a turtleneck sweater. Designed by Suzanne Atkinson.

KNITTED MEASUREMENTS
▦ Neck circumference (closed) 20"/51cm

MATERIALS
▦ 4 1.75oz/50g balls (each approx 137yd/125m) of Filatura Di Crosa/Tahki•Stacy Charles, Inc. *Zara* (100% merino wool) in #1706 dark magenta (₃)
▦ Size 7 (4.5mm) circular needle, 24"/61cm long *or size to obtain gauge*
▦ Cable needle
▦ Stitch markers
▦ Six ⅝"/16mm buttons

GAUGE
32 sts and 32 rows to 4"/10cm worked over yoke chart using size 7 (4.5mm) needle.
Take time to check gauge.

Notes
1 Circular needle is used to accommodate the large number of sts.
2 Neck warmer is worked back and forth in one piece from the top down.
3 Outer collar folds over the under collar.
4 The outer collar buttonholes will be on the edge opposite those of the under collar buttonholes. This allows the neck warmer to button correctly when the outer collar is folded over the under collar.

STITCH GLOSSARY
3-st LPC Sl next 2 sts to cn and hold in *front*, p1, k2 from cn.
3-st RPC Sl next st to cn and hold in *back*, k2, p1 from cn.
4-st LC Sl next 2 sts to cn and hold in *front*, k2, k2 from cn.
4-st RC Sl next 2 sts to cn and hold in *back*, k2, k2 from cn.

SMALL CABLE PATTERN
(over 6 sts)
Row 1 (RS) P1, k4, p1.
Row 2 K1, p4, k1.
Row 3 P1, 4-st LC, p1.
Row 4 Rep row 2.
Rep rows 1–4 for small cable pat.

NECK WARMER
Outer collar
With circular needle, cast on 152 sts. Do not join. Work back and forth as foll:
Set-up row (WS) Wyif, sl 1 purlwise, *k1, p4, k1; rep from * to last st, end k1.
Row 1 (RS) Wyif, sl 1 purlwise, *p1, k4, p1; rep from * to last st, end k1.
Row 2 Wyif, sl 1 purlwise, *k1, p4, k1; rep from * to last st, end k1.
Row 3 Wyif, sl 1 purlwise, *p1, 4-st LC, p1; rep from * to last st, end k1.
Row 4 (buttonhole) Wyif, sl 1 purlwise, k1, p1, bind off next 2 sts, p1, k1, *k1, p4, k1; rep from * to last st, end k1.
Row 5 Wyif, sl 1 purlwise, *p1, k4, p1; rep

from * to 2 sts before bound-off sts, p1, k1, cast on 2 sts over bound-off sts, k1, p1, k1.

Rows 6 and 8 Wyif, sl 1 purlwise, *k1, p4, k1; rep from * to last st, end k1.

Row 7 Wyif, sl 1 purlwise, *p1, 4-st LC, p1; rep from * to last st, end k1.

Row 9 Wyif, sl 1 purlwise, *p1, k4, p1; rep from * to last st, end k1.

Rows 10–17 Rep rows 6–9 twice.

Rows 18–21 Rep rows 2–5.

Rows 22–27 Rep rows 6–9 once, then rows 6 and 7 once more, end with a RS row. Two buttonholes made.

Under collar

Note The next row is the RS of the under collar and yoke.

Rep rows 1–26 as for outer collar, making two more buttonholes.

Row 27 Wyif, sl 1 purlwise, [p1, 4-st LC, p1] twice, *p1, k4, p1, [p1, 4-st LC, p1] twice, p1, k4, p1*, p1, 4-st LC, p1; rep from * to * once, [p1, 4-st LC, p1] 3 times; rep from * to * once, p1, 4-st LC, p1; rep from * to * once, [p1, 4-st LC, p1] twice, k1.

Row 28 Wyif, sl 1 purlwise, *k1, p4, k1; rep from * to last st, end k1.

Yoke

Beg chart pat

Row 1 (RS) Wyif, sl 1 purlwise, [p1, k4, p1] twice, pm, work row 1 of chart over next 24 sts (4 sts inc), pm, p1, k4, p1, pm, work row 1 of chart over next 24 sts (4 sts inc), pm, [p1, k4, p1] 3 times, pm, work row 1 of chart over next 24 sts (4 sts inc), pm, p1, k4, p1, pm, work row 1 of chart over next 24 sts (4 sts inc), pm, [p1, k4, p1] twice, k1—168 sts. Cont to foll chart to row 29. AT THE SAME TIME, cont to work small cable pats beg with row 2, at beg and end of rows as established, and work two more buttonholes when working chart rows 8 and 24. When all rows have been completed, bind off in cable pats.

FINISHING

Block lightly. Sew on buttons.

Yoke Cable

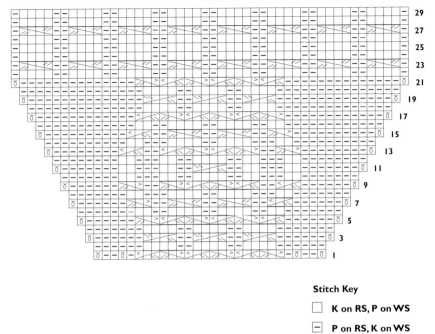

29
27
25
23
21
19
17
15
13
11
9
7
5
3
1

Stitch Key

☐	K on RS, P on WS
⊟	P on RS, K on WS
ŏ	M1 p-st
▷▷>	3-st LPC
<◁◁	3-st RPC
▷▷◁	4-st LC
▷▷◁	4-st RC

Knit a new slant on cabling. Here, simple cables are not only worked on the bias for graphic appeal, but stitches are dropped between them to create an airy fabric. Designed by Helen Hamann.

KNITTED MEASUREMENTS

Approx 8" x 60"/20.5cm x 152.5cm

MATERIALS

- 2 3.5oz/100g balls (each approx 159yd/145m) of Colinette/Unique Kolours *Tagliatelli* (90% merino wool/10% nylon) in #101 monet
- One pair size 11 (8mm) needles *or size to obtain gauge*
- Cable needle

GAUGE

11 sts and 15 rows to 4"/10cm over St st using size 11 (8mm) needles.
Take time to check gauge.

STITCH GLOSSARY

6-st RC Sl next 3 sts to cn and hold in *back*, k3, k3 from cn.

SCARF

Beg at corner, cast on 1 st.
Row 1 (RS) K in front, then back, then front of st—3 sts.
Row 2 P1, k1, p1.
Row 3 K1, M1, p1, M1, k1—5 sts.
Row 4 and all rem WS rows K the knit sts and p the purl sts.
Row 5 K1, M1, k1, p1, k1, M1, k1—7 sts.
Row 7 K1, M1, k2, p1, k2, M1, k1—9 sts.

Row 9 K1, M1, k3, p1, k3, M1, k1—11 sts.
Row 11 K1, M1, k4, p1, k4, M1, k1—13 sts.
Row 13 K1, M1, k5, p1, k5, M1, k1—15 sts.
Row 15 K1, M1, k6, p1, k6, M1, k1—17 sts.
Row 17 K1, M1, p1, 6-st RC, p1, 6-st RC, p1, M1, k1—19 sts.
Row 19 K1, M1, k1, p1, k6, p1, k6, p1, k1, M1, k1—21 sts.
Row 21 K1, M1, k2, p1, k6, p1, k6, p1, k2, M1, k1—23 sts.
Row 23 K1, M1, k3, p1, k6, p1, k6, p1, k3, M1, k1—25 sts.
Row 25 K1, M1, k4, p1, 6-st RC, p1, 6-st RC, p1, k4, M1, k1—27 sts.
Row 27 K1, M1, k5, p1, k6, p1, k6, p1, k5, M1, k1—29 sts
Row 29 K1, M1, k6, p1, k6, p1, k6, p1, k6, M1, k1—31 sts.
Row 31 K1, M1, p1, k6, p1, k6, p1, k6, p1, k6, k2tog—31 sts.

Cont diagonal shaping as established on row 31 (inc at RH edge and dec at LH edge) and incorporating the new inc sts into the cable pat, AT THE SAME TIME, cont to work 6-st RC every 8 rows.

Note When dec a p st between cables, drop this st to the beg. This will count as a dec and will create the ladder effect.

When piece measures 60"/152.5cm (measured along the longer edge), end with a WS row. Beg shaping the opposite corner as foll:

Next row (RS) Ssk, work in cable pat across to last 2 sts (remembering to drop the p st between cables when they are ready for dec), end k2tog. Cont to work in this manner until 3 sts rem, end with a WS row.
Last row (RS) SK2P. Fasten off last st.

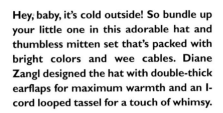

Hey, baby, it's cold outside! So bundle up your little one in this adorable hat and thumbless mitten set that's packed with bright colors and wee cables. Diane Zangl designed the hat with double-thick earflaps for maximum warmth and an I-cord looped tassel for a touch of whimsy.

SIZES

■ Instructions are written for size 3–6 months. Changes for size 6–12 months and 12–18 months are in parentheses.

KNITTED MEASUREMENTS

■ Head circumference 15 (16, 17)"/38 (40.5, 43)cm
■ Hand length 2½ (3, 3½)"/6.5 (7.5, 9)cm

MATERIALS

■ 1 (1, 2) 1.75oz/50g balls (each approx 181yd/166m) of Filatura Di Crosa / Tahki•Stacy Charles, Inc. *Zarina* (100% extrafine merino wool) in #1737 dark lavender (MC) **2**
■ 1 ball in #1758 medium green (CC)

Size 3–6 months
■ One set (4) size 2 (2.75mm) dpn *or size to obtain gauge*

Size 6–12 months
■ One set (4) size 3 (3.25mm) dpn *or size to obtain gauge*

Size 12–18 months
■ One set (4) size 4 (3.5mm) dpn *or size to obtain gauge*
■ Cable needle
■ Stitch markers

GAUGE

Size 3–6 months
28 sts to 4"/10cm over cable pat using size 2 (2.75mm) dpn.

Size 6–12 months
27 sts to 4"/10cm over cable pat using size 3 (3.25mm) dpn.

Size 12–18 months
26 sts to 4"/10cm over cable pat using size 4 (3.5mm) dpn.
Take time to check gauge.

STITCH GLOSSARY

CDD (centered double dec) Sl 2 sts as if to k2tog, k1, pass 2 slipped sts over k st.

TWISTED RIB

(multiple of 2 sts)
Rnd 1 *K1 tbl, p1; rep from * around. Rep this rnd for twisted rib.

CABLE RIB PATTERN

(multiple of 12 sts)
Rnds 1 and 2 *K7, p1, k3, p1; rep from * around.
Rnd 3 *K7, p1, sl next st to cn and hold in *front*, k2, k1 from cn, p1; rep from* around.
Rnds 4–6 Rep rnd 1.
Rep rnds 1–6 for cable rib pat.

HAT

With MC and size 2 (3, 4)/2.75 (3.25, 3.5)mm dpn, cast on 108 sts dividing sts evenly between 3 dpn. Join taking care not to twist sts on dpn. Place marker for end of rnd and sl marker every rnd. Work in twisted rib for 1"/2.5cm. Cont in cable rib pat and work in stripe pat as foll: 3 rnds MC, 2 rnds CC, 4 rnds MC and 2 rnds CC. Cont with MC only until piece measures 3½ (4½, 5½)"/9 (11.5, 14)cm from beg.

Crown shaping

Dec rnd 1 *Ssk, k3, k2tog, p1, cont cable pat over next 3 sts, p1; rep from * around—90 sts. Work next rnd even.

Dec rnd 2 *Ssk, k1, k2tog, p1, cont cable pat over next 3 sts, p1; rep from * around—72 sts. Work next rnd even.

Dec rnd 3 *CDD, p1, cont cable pat over next 3 sts, p1; rep from * around—54 sts. Work next rnd even.

Dec rnd 4 *K1, p1, CDD, p1; rep from * around—36 sts. Work next rnd even.

Dec rnd 5 [K2tog] 18 times—18 sts.

Dec rnd 6 [K2tog] 9 times—9 sts.

I-cord looped tassel

Change to CC and 2 dpn.

Next rnd CDD, [k2tog] 3 times—4 sts. Work I-cord as foll:

*Next row (RS) With 2nd dpn, k4, do not turn. Slide sts back to beg of needle to work next row from RS; rep from * until I-cord measures 6"/15cm from beg.

Last row K4tog—1 st. Cut yarn leaving a 12"/30.5cm tail and pull through rem st. Form three 1"/2.5cm loops at top of hat and sew in place to secure.

With MC and size 2 (3, 4)/2.75 (3.25, 3.5)mm dpn, cast on 18 sts. Work back and forth using 2 dpn as foll:

Row 1 Sl 1, k to end. Rep this row until piece measures 2 (2½, 2¾)"/5 (6.5, 7)cm from beg.

Dec row Sl 1, ssk, k to end—17 sts. Rep this row 13 times more—4 sts.

Tie

Work I-cord as for looped tassel until I-cord measures 8"/20.5cm from beg.

Last row K4tog—1 st. Cut yarn leaving a 6"/15cm tail and pull through rem st. Pull tog tightly and secure end.

On WS, sew cast-on edge of one earflap to last row of twisted rib. On RS, sew bottom edge of twisted rib to earflap. Working in the same manner, sew rem earflap to opposite side of hat.

With MC and size 2 (3, 4)/2.75 (3.25, 3.5)mm dpn, cast on 36 sts dividing sts evenly between 3 dpn. Join taking care not to twist sts on dpn. Place marker for end of rnd and sl marker every rnd. Work in twisted rib for 1"/2.5cm.

Set up rnd K4, pm, p1, k3, p1, pm, knit to end of rnd. Keeping sts between markers in cable pat and rem sts in St st, work for 3 rnds. Work 2 rnds CC, then cont with MC only until piece measures 2 (2½, 3)"/5 (6.5, 7.5)cm from beg.

Top shaping

Dec rnd 1 [K2tog] 18 times—18 sts. Knit next rnd.

Dec rnd 2 [K2tog] 18 times—9 sts. Cut yarn leaving a 6"/15cm tail and thread through rem sts. Pull tog tightly and secure end.

BIAS CABLE HAT

Pinwheel

You're sure to brighten up even the grayest days of winter when you don the this colorful hat. Worked in two vivid contrasting colors, the diagonal stripe pattern is dotted with cable twists. Designed by Diane Zangl.

KNITTED MEASUREMENTS
■ Head circumference 22"/56cm

MATERIALS
■ 1 1.75oz/50g ball (each approx 109yd/100m) of Dale of Norway *Heilo* (100% pure Norwegian wool) each in #6664 teal (A) and #4636 plum (B) ▨
■ Sizes 5 and 6 (3.75 and 4mm) circular needles, 16"/40.5cm long *or size to obtain gauge*
■ One set (4) size 6 (4mm) dpn
■ Two size 5 (3.75mm) dpn (for I-cords)
■ Cable needle
■ Stitch holder
■ Stitch marker

GAUGE
24 sts and 25 rnds to 4"/10cm over striped cable pat using larger circular needle.
Take time to check gauge.

Notes
1 The multiple of sts for the striped cable pat is one more st than the amount of sts cast on. Because there is one less st on needle, the pat will automatically move one st to the left every rnd forming the diagonal stripe. You will not be using a st marker for these rnds, so take extra care to keep track of rnds.
2 When changing colors, pick up new color from under dropped color to prevent holes.
3 Carry color not being used loosely across WS of work.

STITCH GLOSSARY
4-st LC Sl next 2 sts to cn and hold in *front*, k2, k2 from cn.
K2, P2 RIB
(multiple of 4 sts)
Rnd 1 (RS) *K2, p2; rep from * around.
Rep this rnd for k2, p2 rib.

STRIPED CABLE PATTERN
(multiple of 12 sts)
Rnds 1–3 (RS) *With A, k6, with B, k6; rep from * around.
Rnd 4 *With A, k6, with B, k1, 4-st LC, k1; rep from * around.
Rnds 5–8 Rep rnd 1.
Rep rnds 1–8 for striped cable pat.

HAT
With smaller circular needle and A, cast on 132 sts. Join taking care not to twist sts on needle. Place marker for end of rnd and sl marker every rnd. Work in k2, p2 rib for 1½"/4cm, dec 1 st at end of last rnd—131 sts. Drop marker. Change to larger circular needle. Cont in striped cable pat and work until piece measures 7"/17.5cm from beg.

Crown shaping

Note Change to larger dpn (dividing sts evenly between three needles) when there are too few sts on circular needle.

Rnd 1 Keeping to color sequence as established, *k2tog; rep from * around to last st, end k1—66 sts.

Rnd 2 *With A, k3, with B, k3; rep from * around.

Rnd 3 *With A, k1, k2tog, with B, k1, k2tog; rep from * around–44 sts.

Rnd 4 *With A, k2, with B, k2; rep from * around.

Rnd 5 *With A, k2tog, with B, k2tog; rep from * around—22 sts. Cut B.

Rnd 6 With A, [k2tog] 11 times—11 sts.

Rnd 7 With A, [k2tog] 5 times, k1—6 sts. Place first 3 sts on st holder.

I-CORD TASSELS

First tassel

Change to smaller dpn. Work I-cord as foll:
Next row (RS) With 2nd dpn, k3, do not turn. Slide sts back to beg of needle to work next row from RS; rep from * until I-cord measures 2½"/6.5cm from beg. Cut yarn leaving a 6"/15cm tail and thread through rem sts. Pull tog tightly and secure end.

Second tassel

With RS facing, place sts from holder on smaller dpn. Work I-cord same as first tassel for 2"/5cm.

Third tassel

With RS facing, smaller dpn and B, pick up and k 3 sts in center top of hat in front of first tassel. Work I-cord same as first tassel for 2½"/6.5cm.

Fourth tassel

With RS facing, smaller dpn and A, pick up and k 3 sts in center top of hat in front of second tassel. Work I-cord same as first tassel for 3¾"/9.5cm.

Fifth tassel

With RS facing, smaller dpn and B, pick up and k 3 sts in center top of hat between first and second tassels. Work I-cord same as first tassel for 3¼"/8cm.

Sixth tassel

With RS facing, smaller dpn and B, pick up and k 3 sts in center top of hat between third and fourth tassels. Work I-cord same as first tassel for 2¾"/7cm.

Try this new twist on cabling by Norah Gaughan. Knit a pair of mittens that are accented with traveling cables that wrap around and meet on the other side. The cabled lines also provide contrast between the stockinette and reverse stockinette stitches.

KNITTED MEASUREMENTS

■ Hand circumference 7"/17.5cm

MATERIALS

■ 1 3.5oz/100g hank (each approx 174yd/160m) of Berroco, Inc. *Peruvia* (100% Peruvian highland wool) in #7137 granada

(4)

■ One set (4) size 9 (5.5mm) dpn *or size to obtain gauge*

■ Cable needle

■ Stitch markers

GAUGE

18 sts and 24 rnds to 4"/10cm over St st using size 9 (5.5mm) circular needle.
Take time to check gauge.

STITCH GLOSSARY

6-st LC Sl next 3 sts to cn and hold in *front*, k3, k3 from cn.

6-st RC Sl next 3 sts to cn and hold in *back*, k3, k3 from cn.

5-st LC Sl next 2 sts to cn and hold in *front*, k3, k2 from cn.

5-st RC Sl next 3 sts to cn and hold in *back*, k2, k3 from cn.

RIGHT MITTEN

With dpn, cast on 40 sts dividing sts between 3 needles as foll: 13 on first dpn, 14 on 2nd dpn and 13 on 3rd dpn. Join taking care not to twist sts on dpn. Place marker for end of rnd and sl marker every rnd.

Rnds 1–6 P7, k6, p27.

Rnd 7 P7, 6-st LC, p27.

Rnds 8–11 Rep rnd 1.

Thumb gusset

Rnd 12 P7, k6, p7, pm, [M1 p-st] twice, pm, p20—42 sts.

Rnd 13 P7, k6, p7, sl marker, p2, sl marker, p20.

Rnd 14 P7, k6, p7, sl marker, M1 p-st, p2, M1 p-st, sl marker, p20—44 sts.

Rnd 15 P7, k6, p7, sl marker, p4, sl marker, p20.

Rnd 16 P7, k6, p7, sl marker, M1 p-st, p4, M1 p-st, sl marker, p20—46 sts.

Rnd 17 P7, 6-st LC, p7, sl marker, p6, sl marker, p20.

Rnd 18 P7, k6, p7, sl marker, M1 p-st, p6, M1 p-st, sl marker, p20—48 sts.

Rnd 19 P7, k6, p7, sl marker, p8, sl marker, p20.

Rnd 20 P7, k6, p7, sl marker, M1 p-st, p8, M1 p-st, sl marker, p20—50 sts.

Rnd 21 P4, 6-st RC, 6-st LC, p4, sl marker, p10, sl marker, p20.

Rnd 22 P4, k12, p4, sl marker, M1 p-st, p10, M1 p-st, sl marker, p20—52 sts.

Rnd 23 P4, k12, p4, drop marker, place

next 12 sts on waste yarn, drop marker, p20—40 sts.

Hand

Rnd 24 P4, k12, p24. Drop rnd marker.

Rnd 25 P1, 6-st RC, k6, 6-st LC, p21.

Rnd 26 P1, k18, p11, pm, p10. Rnd marker is now at center of palm.

Rnds 27 and 28 P11, k18, p11.

Rnd 29 P8, 6-st RC, k12, 6-st LC, p8.

Rnds 30–32 P8, k24, p8.

Rnd 33 P5, 6-st RC, k18, 6-st LC, p5.

Rnds 34–36 P5, k30, p5.

Rnd 37 P2, 6-st RC, k24, 6-st LC, p2.

Rnds 38–40 P2, k36, p2.

Rnd 41 5-st RC, k30, 5-st LC—cables now meet and there are no more p sts. Drop marker.

Rnd 42 K10, pm. Rnd marker is now at outside edge opposite thumb gusset. Cont in St st on all sts until piece measures 7"/17.5cm from beg.

Top shaping

Dec rnd 1 [Ssk, k16, k2tog] twice—36 sts.

Dec rnd 2 [Ssk, k14, k2tog] twice—32 sts.

Dec rnd 3 [Ssk, k12, k2tog] twice—28 sts.

Dec rnd 4 [Ssk, k10, k2tog] twice—24 sts.

Dec rnd 5 [Ssk, k8, k2tog] twice—20 sts.

Dec rnd 6 [Ssk, k6, k2tog] twice—16 sts.

Dec rnd 7 [Ssk, k4, k2tog] twice—12 sts.

Weave sts tog using Kitchener stitch.

Thumb

P first 4 sts from waste yarn using first dpn, p next 4 sts using 2nd dpn, p last 4 sts using 3rd dpn—12 sts. Place marker for end of rnd and sl marker every rnd. Work around in rev St st for 1¾"/4.5cm.

Top shaping

Dec rnd 1 [P2, p2tog tbl] 3 times—9 sts. Purl next rnd.

Dec rnd 2 [P1, p2tog tbl] 3 times—6 sts. Cut yarn leaving a 6"/15cm tail and thread through rem sts. Pull tog tightly and secure end.

LEFT MITTEN

With dpn, cast on 40 sts dividing sts between 3 needles as foll: 13 on first dpn, 14 on 2nd dpn and 13 on 3rd dpn. Join taking care not to twist sts on dpn. Place marker for end of rnd and sl marker every rnd.

Rnds 1–6 P27, k6, p7.

Rnd 7 P27, 6-st RC, p7.

Rnds 8–11 Rep rnd 1.

Thumb gusset

Rnd 12 P20, pm, [M1 p-st] twice, pm, p7, k6, p7—42 sts.

Rnd 13 P20, sl marker, p2, sl marker, p7, k6, p7.

Rnd 14 P20, sl marker, M1 p-st, p2, M1 p-st, sl marker, p7, k6, p7—44 sts

Rnd 15 P20, sl marker, p4, sl marker, p7, k6, p7.

Rnd 16 P20, sl marker, M1 p-st, p4, M1 p-st, sl marker, p7, k6, p7—46 sts

Rnd 17 P20, sl marker, p6, sl marker, p7, 6-st RC, p7.

Rnd 18 P20, sl marker, M1 p-st, p6, M1 p-st, sl marker, p7, k6, p7—48 sts.

Rnd 19 P20, sl marker, p8, sl marker, p7, k6, p7.

Rnd 20 P20, sl marker, M1 p-st, p8, M1 p-st, sl marker, p7, k6, p7—50 sts.

Rnd 21 P20, sl marker, p10, sl marker, p4, 6-st RC, 6-st LC, p4.

Rnd 22 P20, sl marker, M1 p-st, p10, M1 p-st, sl marker, p4, k12, p4—52 sts.

Rnd 23 P20, drop marker, place next 12 sts on waste yarn, drop marker, p4, k12, p4—20 sts.

Hand

Rnd 24 P24, k12, p4. Drop rnd marker.

Rnd 25 P21, 6-st RC, k6, 6-st LC, p1.

Rnd 26 P10, pm, p11, k18, p1. Rnd marker is now at center of palm.

Rnds 27 and 28 P11, k18, p11.

Rnd 29 P8, 6-st RC, k12, 6-st LC, p8.

Rnds 30–32 P8, k24, p8.

Rnd 33 P5, 6-st RC, k18, 6-st LC, p5.

Rnds 34–36 P5, k30, p5.

Rnd 37 P2, 6-st RC, k24, 6-st LC, p2.

Rnds 38–40 P2, k36, p2.

Rnd 41 5-st RC, k30, 5-st LC—cables now meet and there are no more p sts. Drop marker.

Rnd 42 K30, pm. Rnd marker is now at outside edge opposite thumb gusset. Cont in St st on all sts until piece measures 7"/17.5cm from beg. Work top shaping and thumb as for right mitten.

You never need to sacrifice fashion for warmth when you wrap yourself in Fiona Ellis' beautiful scarf. It's adorned with a stunning variation of the classic horse-shoe cable, sweet hugs and kisses cables, and graceful ribbed borders.

KNITTED MEASUREMENTS
■ Approx 14" x 54"/35.5cm x 137cm

MATERIALS
■ 6 3.5oz/100g balls (each approx 218yd/200m) of Nashua Handknits/Westminster Fibers, Inc. *Creative Focus Superwash* (50% superwash wool/50% superwash merino) in #29 charcoal **(4)**
■ One pair each size 7 and 8 (4.5 and 5mm) needles *or size to obtain gauge*
■ Cable needle

GAUGE
18 sts and 26 rows to 4"/10cm over St st using smaller needles. *Take time to check gauge.*

STITCH GLOSSARY
6-st RC Sl next 3 sts to cn and hold in *back*, k3, k3 from cn.
6-st LC Sl next 3 sts to cn and hold in *front*, k3, k3 from cn.
8-st RC Sl next 4 sts to cn and hold in *back*, k4, k4 from cn.
8-st LC Sl next 4 sts to cn and hold in *front*, k4, k4 from cn.

CABLE PATTERN A
(over 12 sts)
Rows 1, 5, 7, 11, 13, 17, 19, 23 (RS) K12.
Row 2 and all WS rows P12.
Rows 3 and 9 6-st RC, 6-st LC.
Rows 15 and 21 6-st LC, 6-st RC.
Row 24 P12.
Rep rows 1–24 for cable pat A.

CABLE PATTERN B
(over 16 sts)
Rows 1, 5, 7, 11 (RS) K16.
Row 2 and all WS rows P16.
Row 3 8-st RC, k8.
Row 9 K8, 8-st LC.
Row 12 P16.
Rep rows 1–12 for cable pat B.

SIDE PANEL PATTERN
(over 12 sts)
Row 1 P1, k1, p2tog, p1, [k1, p1] 3 times, M1, k1.
Row 2 P2, [k1, p1] 3 times, k2, p1, k1.
Row 3 P1, k1, p2tog, [k1, p1] 3 times, k1, M1 p-st, k1.
Row 4 [P1, k1] 6 times.
Rep rows 1–4 for side panel pat.

SCARF
With larger needles, cast on 87 sts.
Set-up row 1 (WS) K1, *p1, k1; rep from * to end.

Set-up row 2 (RS) K1, *p1, k1, p3, [k1, p1] 7 times, k1, p3, k1; rep from * twice more, end p1, k1, p3, [k1, p1] 3 times, k1, p1, k1.

Set-up row 3 (WS) K2, [p1, k1] 3 times, p1, k3, p1, k1, *p1, k3, [p1, k1] 7 times, p1, k3, p1, k1; rep from * twice more, end k1.

Beg lower border pat

Row 1 (RS) K1, *p1, k1, p2tog, p1, [k1, p1] 3 times, M1, k1, p1, k1, M1, p1, [k1, p1] 3 times, p2tog, k1; rep from * twice more, end p1, k1, p2tog, p1, [k1, p1] 3 times, M1, k1, p1, k1.

Row 2 K2, p2, [k1, p1] 3 times, k2, p1, k1, *p1, k2, [p1, k1] 3 times, p2, k1, p2, [k1, p1] 3 times, k2, p1, k1; rep from * twice more, end k1.

Row 3 K1, *p1, k1, p2tog, [k1, p1] 3 times, k1, M1 p-st, k1, p1, k1, M1 p-st, [k1, p1] 3 times, k1, p2tog, k1; rep from * twice more, end p1, k1, p2tog, [k1, p1] 3 times, k1, M1 p-st, k1, p1, k1.

Row 4 K2, [p1, k1] to last st, end k1. Rep rows 1–4 until piece measures 3"/7.5cm from beg, end with row 4. Change to smaller needles.

Beg cable and side panel pats

Set-up row (RS) K1, work row 1 of side panel pat over next 12 sts, p1, p2tog, p1, work row 1 of cable pat A over next 12 sts, p2, p2tog, p2, work row 1 of cable pat B over next 16 sts, p2, p2tog, p2, work row 1 of cable pat A over next 12 sts, p1, p2tog, p1, work row 1 of side panel pat over next 12 sts, p1, k1—83 sts.

Next row (WS) K2, work row 2 of side panel pat, k3, work row 2 of cable pat A, k5, work row 2 of cable pat B, k5, work row 2 of cable pat A, k3, work row 2 of side panel pat, k1.

Next row (RS) K1, work row 3 of side panel pat, p3, work row 3 of cable pat A, p5, work row 3 of cable pat B, p5, work row 3 of cable pat A, p3, work row 3 of side panel pat, p1, k1. Cont in pats as established until piece measures 51"/129.5cm, end with row 4 of side panel pat as foll:

Next row (WS) K2, work row 4 of side panel pat, k1, M1, k2, work cable pat A, k2, M1, k3, work cable pat B, k3, M1, k2, work cable pat A, k2, M1, k1, work row 4 of side panel pat, k1—87 sts. Change to larger needles. Rep rows 1–4 of lower border pat until piece measures 54"/137cm from beg, end with a WS row. Bind off in k1, p1 rib.

Block lightly to measurements.

Lower Border Pattern

24-st rep

Cable Pattern A

Cable Pattern B

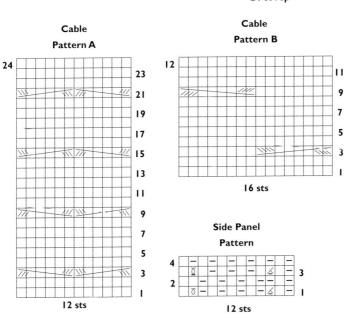

12 sts

16 sts

Side Panel Pattern

12 sts

Stitch Key

☐	**K on RS, p on WS**	6-st RC
−	**P on RS, k on WS**	6-st LC
⟋	**P2tog**	8-st RC
ठ	**M1**	8-st LC
⟋	**M1 p st**	

59

Chained melody

Hats off to Norah Gaughan for designing this fun traveling cable cap. The cables advance with every twist, creating a swirl of texture around your head.

KNITTED MEASUREMENTS

■ Head circumference 18"/45.5cm

MATERIALS

■ 1 3.5oz/100g hank (each approx 174yd/160m) of Berroco, Inc. *Peruvia* (100% Peruvian highland wool) in #7135 caliente **(4)**

■ Size 9 (5.5mm) circular needle, 16"/40.5cm long *or size to obtain gauge*

■ One set (4) size 9 (5.5mm) dpn

■ Cable needle

■ Stitch marker

GAUGE

18 sts and 24 rnds to 4"/10cm over St st using size 9 (5.5mm) circular needle. *Take time to check gauge.*

STITCH GLOSSARY

8-st RPC Sl next 5 sts to cn and hold in *back*, k3, (k3, p2) from cn.

6-st RC Sl next 3 sts to cn and hold in *back*, k3, k3 from cn.

HAT

With circular needle, cast on 96 sts. Join taking care not to twist sts on needle. Place marker for end of rnd and sl marker every rnd.

Rnds 1–5 *P6, k6; rep from * around.

Rnd 6 *P4, 8-st RPC; rep from * around.

Rnds 7–15 *P4, k6, p2; rep from * around.

Rnd 16 *P2, 8-st RPC, p2; rep from * around.

Rnds 17–25 *P2, k6, p4; rep from * around.

Rnd 26 *8-st RPC, p4; rep from * around.

Crown shaping

Note Change to dpn (dividing sts evenly between three needles) when there are too few sts on circular needle.

Rnd (dec) 27 *K6, p2tog, p4; rep from * around—88 sts.

Rnds 28–33 *K6, p5; rep from * around.

Rnd (dec) 34 *K6, p2tog, p3; rep from * around—80 sts.

Rnd 35 *K6, p4; rep from * around.

Rnd 36 *6-st RC, p4; rep from * around.

Rnd (dec) 37 *K6, p2tog, p2; rep from * around—72 sts.

Rnd (dec) 38 *K5, k2tog, p2—64 sts.

Rnd (dec) 39 *K5, k2tog, p1—56 sts.

Rnd (dec) 40 *K5, k2tog—48 sts.

Rnd (dec) 41 *K4, k2tog—40 sts.

Rnd (dec) 42 *K3, k2tog—32 sts.

Rnd (dec) 43 *K2, k2tog—24 sts.

Rnd (dec) 44 *K1, k2tog—16 sts.

Rnd (dec) 45 [K2tog] 8 times—8 sts. Cut yarn leaving a 8"/20.5cm tail and thread through rem sts. Pull tog tightly and secure end.

Alpine for you

Cozy up to something cabled. Simona Merchant-Dest's chill-chasing hood with attached scarf is packed with richly textured cables. Cables create a double-thick fabric, making them extra-warm.

KNITTED MEASUREMENTS
- Hood 10½" x 13½"/26.5cm x 34cm
- Scarf 8½" x 60"/21.5cm x 152.5cm

MATERIALS
- 10 1.75oz/50g balls (each approx 95yd/87m) of RYC/Westminster Fibers, Inc. *Cashsoft Aran* (57% extrafine merino/33% microfiber/10% cashmere) in #1oat (**4**)
- One pair size 8 (5mm) needles *or size to obtain gauge*
- Cable needle
- Stitch markers

GAUGES
- 19 sts and 26 rows to 4"/10cm over St st using size 8 (5mm) needles.
- 28 sts and 26 rows to 4"/10cm over chart A using size 8 (5mm) needles.
- 25 sts and 26 rows to 4"/10cm over chart B using size 8 (5mm) needles.

Take time to check gauges.

STITCH GLOSSARY
4-st LC Sl next 2 sts to cn and hold in *front*, k2, k2 from cn.

4-st RC Sl next 2 sts to cn and hold in *back*, k2, k2 from cn.

4-st LPC Sl next 2 sts to cn and hold in *front*, p2, k2 from cn.

4-st RPC Sl next 2 sts to cn and hold in *back*, k2, p2 from cn.

K2, P2 RIB
(multiple of 4 sts plus 2)

Row 1 (RS) K2, *p2, k2; rep from * to end.

Row 2 P2, *k2, p2; rep from * to end.

Rep rows 1 and 2 for k2, p2 rib.

SCARF (MAKE 2 PIECES)
Beg at bottom edge, cast on 54 sts. Work in k2, p2 rib for 4 rows.

Beg chart pats

Row 1 (RS) Work row 1 of chart A over 14 sts, pm, work row 1 of chart B over 26 sts, pm, work row 1 of chart C over 14 sts. Cont to foll charts A and C to row 4, then rep rows 1–4 to the end. AT THE SAME TIME, cont to foll chart B to row 34, then *rep rows 1–20 twice, then rows 21–34 once; rep from * once more, then rep rows 1–20 twice; piece should measure approx 30"/76cm from beg. Bind off in cable pat.

HOOD (MAKE 2 PIECES)
Beg at bottom edge, cast on 62 sts. Purl next row.

Beg chart pats

Row 1 (RS) Work row 1 of chart D over 18 sts, pm, work row 1 of chart B over 26 sts, pm, work row 1 of chart E over 18 sts. Cont to foll charts D and E to row 4, then rep rows 1–4 to the end. AT THE SAME TIME, cont to foll chart B to row 34, then rep rows 1–20 twice. Beg with row 21, work even until piece measures 13"/33cm from beg, end with a WS row. Bind off in cable pat.

FINISHING

Sew bound-off edges of scarf pieces tog. Sew bound-off edges of hood pieces tog for top seam. Fold hood in half along top seam so RS are facing. Sew side edges of hood tog for back seam. Line up scarf seam with back seam of hood. Sew bottom edge of hood to edge of scarf.

Pompom

Make a 2½"/6.5cm diameter pompom and sew to peak of hood.

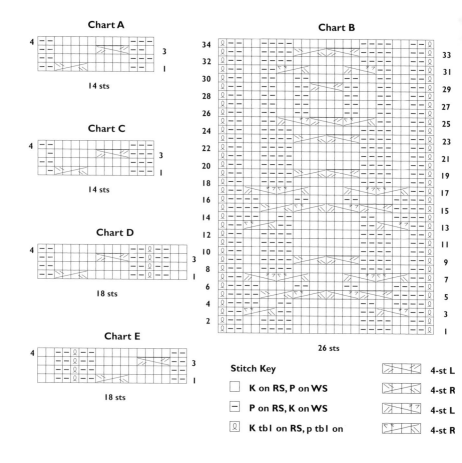

Chart A · 14 sts · Chart B · 26 sts · Chart C · 14 sts · Chart D · 18 sts · Chart E · 18 sts

Stitch Key

☐ K on RS, P on WS
— P on RS, K on WS
Ω K tbl on RS, p tbl on

4-st L
4-st R
4-st L
4-st R

Sassy stripes

6-st RC Sl next 3 sts to cn and hold in *back*, k3, k3 from cn.

6-st LPC Sl next 3 sts to cn and hold in *front*, p3, k3 from cn.

6-st RPC Sl next 3 sts to cn and hold in *back*, k3, p3 from cn.

■■■■▶

Get set for the season with Christine Walter's warm and wonderful headband and mittens. The ensemble is styled with wide cabled bands, mini stripes and novel I-cord knotted buttons.

KNITTED MEASUREMENTS

■ Head circumference 21"/53.5cm
■ Hand circumference 7½"/19cm

MATERIALS

■ 2 3.5oz/100g balls (each approx 166yd/152m) of Moda Dea/Coats & Clark *Washable Wool* (100% merino wool superwash) in #4441 lake blue (MC) **4**
■ 1 ball each in #4418 real teal (A) and #4435 taupe (B)
■ One pair size 8 (5mm) needles *or size to obtain gauge*
■ One set (4) each size 7 (4.5 and 5mm) dpn *or size to obtain gauge*
■ Cable needle
■ Stitch markers

GAUGES

■ 25 sts to 3¼"/8cm and 27 rows to 4"/10cm over cable band using size 8 (5mm) needles.
■ 18 sts and 28 rows to 4"/10cm over St st using size 7 (4.5mm) dpn.
Take time to check gauges.

STITCH GLOSSARY

6-st LC Sl next 3 sts to cn and hold in *front*, k3, k3 from cn.

CABLE BAND PATTERN

(over 25 sts)

Row 1 (RS) K2, 6-st LC, p6, 6-st LPC, k5.
Row 2 K2, p6, k9, p6, k2.
Row 3 K5, 6-st LC, p6, 6-st LPC, k2.
Row 4 K2, p3, k9, p9, k2.
Row 5 K8, 6-st LC, p6, k5.
Row 6 K2, p3, k6, p12, k2.
Row 7 K11, 6-st LPC, p3, k5.
Row 8 K2, [p3, k3] twice, p9, k2.
Row 9 K5, 6-st RC, p3, k3, 6-st RC, k2.
Row 10 K2, p9, k3, p9, k2.
Row 11 K2, 6-st RPC, k3, p3, 6-st RC, k5.
Row 12 K2, p9, [k3, p3] twice, k2.
Row 13 K5, p3, 6-st LPC, k11.
Row 14 K2, p12, k6, p3, k2.
Row 15 K5, p6, 6-st LPC, k8.
Row 16 K2, p9, k9, p3, k2.
Rep rows 1–16 for cable band pat.

STRIPE PATTERN

*2 rows B, 2 rows MC, 2 rows A; rep from * (6 rows) for stripe pat.

HEADBAND

With larger straight needles and MC, cast on 25 sts.

Set up row (WS) K2, p9, k9, p3, k2. Cont in cable band pat, rep rows 1–16 8 times, then rows 1–15 once more; piece should measure approx 21"/53.5cm from beg. Do not bind off.

FINISHING

Graft sts on needle to cast-on edge, taking care to match k sts and p sts.

RIGHT MITTEN

Cuff

With larger straight needles and MC, cast on 18 sts. Knit next 7 rows for buttonband.

Next (inc) row (RS) K2, k in front and back of next st, [k1, k in front and back of next st] 6 times, k3—25 sts.

Set up row (WS) K2, p9, k9, p3, k2. Cont in cable band pat, rep rows 1–16 3 times.

Next (dec) row (RS) K3, k2tog, [k1, k2tog] 6 times, k2—18 sts. Knit next 3 rows.

Buttonhole row (RS) K3, [wyif, k2tog, k3] 3 times. Knit next 2 rows. Bind off all sts knitwise.

Hand

Position cuff so RS is facing and buttonhole band is at right. With dpn and A, pick up and k 4 sts across side edge of buttonhole band, cont to pick up and k 29 sts across side edge of cuff to buttonband, dividing sts evenly between 3 needles—33 sts. Place marker for end of rnd and sl marker every rnd.

Next (inc) rnd K, inc 2 sts evenly spaced—35 sts. Cont in St st and stripe pat as foll:

Thumb gusset

Inc rnd 1 K 17 sts, pm, M1, k1, M1, pm, k to end—37 sts (3 thumb gusset sts between markers). Knit next 2 rnds.

Inc rnd 2 K to marker, sl marker, M1, k3, M1, k to end—5 thumb gusset sts. Knit next 2 rnds.

Inc rnd 3 K to marker, sl marker, M1, k5, M1, k to end—7 thumb gusset sts. Knit next 3 rnds.

Inc rnd 4 K to marker, sl marker, M1, k7, M1, k to end—9 thumb gusset sts. Knit next 3 rnds.

Inc rnd 5 K to marker, sl marker, M1, k9, M1, k to end—11 thumb gusset sts. Knit next rnd.

Next rnd K to marker, drop marker, place next 11 sts on waste yarn, drop marker, cast on 1 st, k to end—35 sts. Work even until piece measures 8¾"/22cm from beg (including cuff).

Top shaping

Dec rnd 1 [K7, k2tog] 3 times, k8—32 sts.

Dec rnd 2 [K6, k2tog] 4 times—28 sts. Knit next rnd

Dec rnd 3 [K5, k2tog] 4 times—24 sts. Knit next rnd.

Dec rnd 4 [K4, k2tog] 4 times—20 sts. Knit next rnd.

Dec rnd 5 [K3, k2tog] 4 times—16 sts.

Dec rnd 6 [K2, k2tog] 4 times—12 sts.

Dec rnd 7 [K1, k2tog] 4 times—8 sts. Cut yarn leaving a 6"/15cm tail and thread through rem sts. Pull tog tightly and secure end.

Thumb

Cont stripe pat as established, k first 4 sts from waste yarn using first dpn, k next 4 sts using 2nd dpn, k last 3 sts using 3rd dpn, then pick up and knit 1 st in cast-on st—12 sts. Place marker for end of rnd and sl marker every rnd. Work even for 1¾"/4.5cm.

Top shaping

Dec rnd 1 [K2, k2tog] 3 times—9 sts. Knit next rnd.

Dec rnd 2 [K1, k2tog] 3 times—6 sts. Cut yarn leaving a 6"/15cm tail and thread through rem sts. Pull tog tightly and secure end.

LEFT MITTEN

Work as for right mitten to hand.

Hand

Position cuff so RS is facing and buttonband is at right. With dpn and A, skip buttonband, then pick up and k 29 sts across side edge of cuff to buttonhole band, pick up and k 4 sts across side edge of buttonhole band, dividing sts evenly between 3 needles—33 sts. Place marker for end of rnd and sl marker every rnd. Cont to work as for right mitten.

FINISHING

For each mitten, lap buttonband under buttonhole band and sew top side edge in place.

I-cord buttons (make 6 pieces)

With dpn and B, cast on 3 sts leaving a long tail for sewing. Work I-cord as foll:

*Next row (RS) With 2nd dpn, k3, do not turn. Slide sts back to beg of needle to work next row from RS; rep from * until I-cord measures 3"/7.5cm from beg. Bind off as foll: k1, k2tog, pass first st over 2nd st. Cut yarn leaving an 8"/20.5cm tail and thread through rem st. Pull tog tightly and secure end; do not cut tail. Tie each I-cord in a loose knot, then fold one end under to form a ball shape. Use tails to secure knot; do not cut tails. Use tails to sew on buttons.

Cable Band
(25 sts)

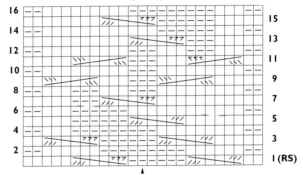

STITCH KEY

☐ K on RS, P on WS

— P on RS, K on WS

6-st LC

6-st LPC

6-st RC

6-st RPC

Vanessa Montileone's cap-tivating double moss stitch hat is sheer perfection. The brim is embellished with a graceful open cable dotted with dainty bobbles, as well a slip-stitch edging that creats a flawless finish.

KNITTED MEASUREMENTS
■ Head circumference 22"/56cm

MATERIALS
■ 1 4oz/113g hank (each approx 225yd/206m) of Lorna's Laces *Shepherd Worsted* (100% superwash wool) each in #74 motherlode (A) and #2ns manzanita (B) ⬛4⬛
■ One pair size 7 (4.5mm) needles *or size to obtain gauge*
■ Size 7 (4.5mm) circular needle, 16"/40.5cm long
■ One set (4) size 7 (4.5mm) dpn
■ Cable needle
■ Stitch marker

GAUGE
22 sts and 28 rows to 4"/10cm over St st using size 7 (4.5mm) needles.
Take time to check gauge.

Note
Cabled brim is worked back and forth in rows and the crown is worked in rnds.

STITCH GLOSSARY
4-st RPC Sl next st to cn and hold in *back*, k3, p1 from cn.

4-st LPC Sl next 3 sts to cn and hold in *front*, p1, k3 from cn.

7-st RPC Sl next 4 sts to cn and hold in *back*, k3, sl last st on cn to LH needle and p it, k3 from cn.

MB (bobble) In same st work k1, [p1, k1] twice; turn, k5; turn, p5; pass the 2nd, 3rd, 4th, then 5th sts over the first st.

DOUBLE MOSS STITCH
(multiple of 4 sts)
Rnds 1 and 2 *K2, p2; rep from * around.
Rnds 3 and 4 *P2, k2; rep from * around.
Rep rnds 1–4 for double moss st.

HAT
Cabled brim
With straight needles and A, cast on 19 sts using a provisional cast-on (optional).
Row 1 (WS) P2, k4, p3, k1, p3, k4, sl last 2 sts to RH needle purlwise.
Row 2 K2, p4, 7-st RPC, p4, sl last 2 sts to RH needle purlwise.
Row 3 Rep row 1.
Row 4 K2, p3, 4-st RPC, p1, 4-st LPC, p3, sl last 2 sts to RH needle purlwise.
Row 5 P2, k3, p3, k3, p3, k3, sl last 2 sts to RH needle purlwise.
Row 6 K2, p2, 4-st RPC, p3, 4-st LPC, p2, sl last 2 sts to RH needle purlwise.
Row 7 P2, k2, p3, k5, p3, k2, sl last 2 sts to RH needle purlwise.
Row 8 K2, p2, k3, p2, MB, p2, k3, p2, sl last 2 sts to RH needle purlwise.

Row 9 Rep row 7.

Row 10 K2, p2, 4-st LPC, p3, 4-st RPC, p2, sl last 2 sts to RH needle purlwise.

Row 11 Rep row 5.

Row 12 K2, p3, 4-st LPC, p1, 4-st RPC, p3, sl last 2 sts to RH needle purlwise.

Row 13 Rep row 1.

Row 14 Rep row 2.

Row 15 Rep row 1.

Row 16 Rep row 4.

Row 17 Rep row 5.

Row 18 Rep row 6.

Row 19 Rep row 7.

Row 20 K2, p2, k3, p5, k3, p2, sl last 2 sts to RH needle purlwise.

Row 21 Rep row 7.

Row 22 Rep row 10.

Row 23 Rep row 5.

Row 24 Rep row 12. Rep rows 1–24 6 times more. Sew cast-on edge to bound-off edge forming a ring. Or, for provisional cast-on option, weave sts tog using Kitchener stitch.

Crown

With RS facing, B and circular needle, pick up and k 120 sts along one edge of cabled brim, beg and ending at seam (or joined sts). Place marker for end of rnd and sl marker every rnd. Work around in double moss st until piece measures 5"/12.5cm from beg (including cabled brim).

Crown shaping

Notes When dec, maintain double moss st by working either a k2tog or p2tog. Change to dpn (dividing sts evenly between three needles) when there are too few sts on circular needle.

Dec rnd 1 *Work double moss st over next 13 sts, work next 2 sts tog; rep from * around—112 sts. Work next rnd even.

Dec rnd 2 *Work double moss st over next 12 sts, work next 2 sts tog; rep from * around—104 sts. Work next rnd even.

Dec rnd 3 *Work double moss st over next 11 sts, work next 2 sts tog; rep from * around—96 sts. Work next rnd even.

Dec rnd 4 *Work double moss st over next 10 sts, work next 2 sts tog; rep from * around— 88 sts. Work next rnd even. Cont to work dec rnds as established, with one less st between decs, until 16 sts rem.

Next rnd [K2tog] 8 times—8 sts.

Next rnd [K2tog] 4 times—4 sts. Cut yarn leaving a 8"/20.5cm tail and thread through rem sts. Pull tog tightly and secure end.

Cabled Brim
(19 sts)

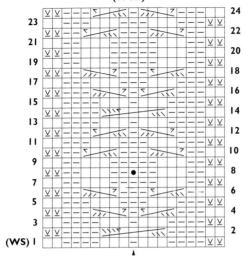

STITCH KEY

☐ K on RS, P on WS

⊟ P on RS, K on WS

Ⅴ Sl st purlwise

4-st RPC

4-st LPC

7-st RPC

● MB (bobble)

Guinevere

This enchanting piece is super-functional, yet carries a hint of dramatic flair. Linda Cyr has adorned this helmet-style hat with attached scarf, with two sizes of the same classic cable pattern, giving it timeless appeal.

KNITTED MEASUREMENTS
- Head circumference 21"/53.5cm
- Scarf 5" x 72"/12.5cm x 183cm

MATERIALS
- 6 1.5oz/40g balls (each approx 84yd/71m) of Lion Brand Yarn *Lion Cashmere Blend* (72% merino wool/15% nylon/13% cashmere) in #98 cream (**4**)
- One pair size 8 (5mm) needles *or size to obtain gauge*
- Sizes 8 and 10 (5 and 6mm) circular needles, 16"/40.5cm long
- One set (4) size 8 (5mm) dpn
- Cable needle
- Stitch marker

GAUGE
20 sts and 24 rows to 4"/10cm over St st using size 8 (5mm) needles.
Take time to check gauge.

Note
Helmet cable band is worked back and forth in rows and the crown is worked in rnds.

STITCH GLOSSARY
3-st RPC Sl next st to cn and hold in *back*, k2, p1, from cn.

3-st LPC Sl next 2 sts to cn and hold in *front*, p1, k2 from cn.

4-st RC Sl 2 next sts to cn and hold in *back*, k2, k2 from cn.

LARGE DIAMOND CABLE
(over 16 sts)
Row 1 (RS) P6, k4, p6.
Row 2 and all WS rows K the knit sts and p the purl sts.
Row 3 P6, 4-st RC, p6.
Row 5 P5, 3-st RPC, 3-st LPC, p5.
Row 7 P4, 3-st RPC, p2, 3-st LPC, p4.
Row 9 P3, 3-st RPC, p4, 3-st LPC, p3.
Row 11 P2, 3-st RPC, p6, 3-st LPC, p2.
Row 13 P1, 3-st RPC, p8, 3-st LPC, p1.
Row 15 3-st RPC, p10, 3-st LPC.
Row 17 3-st LPC, p10, 3-st RPC.
Row 19 P1, 3-st LPC, p8, 3-st RPC, p1.
Row 21 P2, 3-st LPC, p6, 3-st RPC, p2.
Row 23 P3, 3-st LPC, p4, 3-st RPC, p3.
Row 25 P4, 3-st LPC, p2, 3-st RPC, p4.
Row 27 P5, 3-st LPC, 3-st RPC, p5.
Row 29 P6, 4-st RC, p6.
Row 30 Rep row 2.
Rep rows 1–30 for large diamond cable.

SMALL DIAMOND CABLE
(over 10 sts)
Row 1 (RS) P3, k4, p3.

Row 2 and all WS rows K the knit sts and p the purl sts.

Row 3 P3, 4-st RC, p3.

Row 5 P2, 3-st RPC, 3-st LPC, p2.

Row 7 P1, 3-st RPC, p2, 3-st LPC, p1.

Row 9 3-st RPC, p4, 3-st LPC.

Row 11 3-st LPC, p4, 3-st RPC.

Row 13 P1, 3-st LPC, p2, 3-st RPC, p1.

Row 15 P2, 3-st LPC, 3-st RPC, p2.

Row 17 P3, 4-st RC, p3.

Row 18 Rep row 2.

Rep rows 1–18 for small diamond cable.

With straight needles, cast on 24 sts.

Border pat

Rows 1–6 Wyib, sl 1 purlwise, k to end.

Beg cable pat

Row 1 (RS) Wyib, sl 1 purlwise, k2, p1, pm, work row 1 of large diamond cable over 16 sts, pm, p1, k3.

Row 2 Wyib, sl 1 purlwise, k3, work row 2 of large diamond cable over 16 sts, k4. Cont in pats as established until 14 reps have been completed, end with a WS row. Rep rows 1–6 of border pat once more. Bind off all sts knitwise.

Cable band

With straight needles, cast on 16 sts.

Beg cable pat

Row 1 (RS) Wyib, sl 1 purlwise, k1, p1, pm, work row 1 of small diamond cable over 10 sts, pm, p1, k2.

Row 2 Wyib, sl 1 purlwise, k2, work row 2 of small diamond cable over 10 sts, k3. Cont in pats as established until 7 reps have been completed, end with a WS row. Bind off. Sew cast-on edge to bound-off edge forming a ring.

Crown

With WS facing and larger circular needle, pick up and k 63 sts along one side edge of cable band, beg and ending at seam.

Inc rnd (RS) With RS facing and smaller circular needle, *k3, M1; rep from * around—84 sts. Place marker for end of rnd and sl marker every rnd. Work around in St st until piece measures 7½"/19cm from beg (including cable band).

Crown shaping

Note Change to dpn (dividing sts evenly between three needles) when there are too few sts on circular needle.

Dec rnd 1 *K10, k2tog; rep from * around—77 sts.

Next rnd Knit.

Dec rnd 2 *K9, k2tog; rep from * around—70 sts.

Next rnd Knit.

Dec rnd 3 *K8, k2tog; rep from * around—63 sts.

Next rnd Knit.

Dec rnd 4 *K7, k2tog; rep from * around—56 sts.

Next rnd Knit.

Dec rnd 5 *K6, k2tog; rep from * around—49 sts.

Next rnd Knit.

Dec rnd 6 *K5, k2tog; rep from * around—42 sts.

Next rnd Knit.

Dec rnd 7 *K4, k2tog; rep from * around—35 sts.

Next rnd Knit.

Dec rnd 8 *K3, k2tog; rep from * around—28 sts.

Next rnd Knit.

Dec rnd 9 *K2, k2tog; rep from * around—21 sts.

Next rnd Knit.

Dec rnd 10 *K1, k2tog; rep from * around—14 sts.

Next rnd Knit.

Dec rnd 11 [K2tog] 7 times—7 sts. Cut yarn leaving a 8"/20.5cm tail and thread through rem sts. Pull tog tightly and secure end.

FINISHING

Steam-block scarf to measurements. Measure and mark center of one long edge of scarf. Line up center of scarf with center back seam of helmet. Sew bottom edge of helmet to edge of scarf for 5"/12.5cm on either side of center back seam.

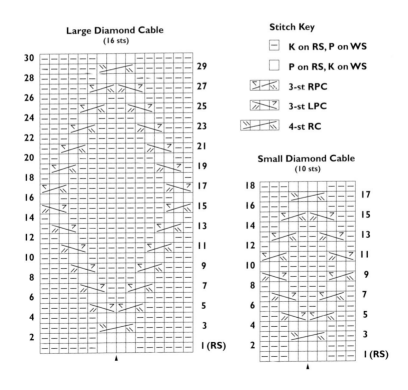

Large Diamond Cable
(16 sts)

Stitch Key

⊟ K on RS, P on WS

☐ P on RS, K on WS

3-st RPC

3-st LPC

4-st RC

Small Diamond Cable
(10 sts)

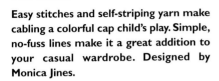

Easy stitches and self-striping yarn make cabling a colorful cap child's play. Simple, no-fuss lines make it a great addition to your casual wardrobe. Designed by Monica Jines.

KNITTED MEASUREMENTS
■ Head circumference 19½"/49.5cm

MATERIALS
■ 2 1.75oz/50g balls (each approx 110yd/101m) of Classic Elite Yarns *Desert* (100% wool) in #2027 tumbleweed (4)
■ Size 7 (4.5mm) circular needle, 16"/40cm long *or size to obtain gauge*
■ One set (4) size 7 (4.5mm) dpn
■ Cable needle
■ Stitch marker

GAUGE
22 sts and 27 rnds to 4"/10cm over cable pat using size 7 (4.5mm) circular needle.
Take time to check gauge.

STITCH GLOSSARY
4-st LC Sl next 2 sts to cn and hold in *front*, k2, k2 from cn.

CABLE PATTERN
(multiple of 12 sts)
Rnds 1 and 2 (RS) *P2, k4; rep from * around.
Rnd 3 *P2, 4-st LC, p2, k4; rep from * around.
Rnds 4 and 5 Rep rnd 1.
Rep rnds 1–5 for cable pat.

HAT
With circular needle, cast on 108 sts. Join taking care not to twist sts on needle. Place marker for end of rnd and sl marker every rnd. Work in cable pat, rep rnds 1–5 7 times.
Crown shaping
Note Change to dpn (dividing sts evenly between three needles) when there are too few sts on circular needle.
Rnd 1 *P2, k4, p2, k2, k2tog; rep from * around—99 sts.
Rnd 2 *P2, k4, p2, k3; rep from * around.
Rnd 3 *P2, 4-st LC, p2, k1, k2tog; rep from * around—90 sts.
Rnd 4 *P2, k4, p2, k2; rep from * around.
Rnd 5 *P2, k4, p2, k2tog; rep from * around—81 sts.
Rnd 6 *P2, k4, p2, k1; rep from * around.
Rnd 7 *P2, k4, p1, k2tog; rep from * around—72 sts.
Rnd 8 *P2, 4-st LC, p1, k1; rep from * around.
Rnd 9 *P2, k4, k2tog; rep from * around—63 sts.
Rnd 10 *P2, k5; rep from * around.
Rnd 11 *P2, k3, k2tog; rep from * around—54 sts.
Rnd 12 *P2, k2, k2tog; rep from * around—45 sts.
Rnd 13 *P2, k1, k2tog; rep from * around—36 sts.
Rnd 14 *P2, k2tog; rep from * around—27 sts.
Rnd 15 *P1, k2tog; rep from * around—18 sts.
Rnd 16 [K2tog] 9 times—9 sts. Cut yarn leaving a 8"/20.5cm tail and thread through rem sts. Pull tog tightly and secure end.

POMPOM HAT

Fisherman's pride

6-st LC Sl next 3 sts to cn and hold in *front*, k3, k3 from cn.

CABLE RIB

(multiple of 4 sts plus 2)

Row 1 (RS) P2, *2-st RT, p2; rep from * to end.

Row 2 K2, *p2, k2; rep from * to end.

Rep rows 1 and 2 for cable rib.

CABLE PANEL A

(over 4 sts)

Row 1 (RS) K4.

Row 2 P4.

Row 3 4-st LC.

Row 4 P4.

Rep rows 1–4 for cable panel A.

CABLE PANEL B

(over 22 sts)

Row 1 (RS) P4, 3-st RC, p1, 6-st LC, p1, 3-st LC, p4.

Row 2 K4, p2, k1, p8, k1, p2, k4.

Row 3 P3, 3-st RPC, k1, p1, k6, p1, k1, 3-st LPC, p3.

Row 4 K3, p3, k1, p8, k1, p3, k3.

Row 5 P2, 3-st RC, p1, k1, p1, k6, p1, k1, p1, 3-st LC, p2.

Row 6 K2, p2, k1, p1, k1, p8, k1, p1, k1, p2, k2.

Row 7 P1, 3-st RPC, [k1, p1] twice, 6-st LC, [p1, k1] twice, 3-st LPC, p1.

Row 8 K1, p3, k1, p1, k1, p8, k1, p1, k1, p3, k1.

Row 9 P1, 3-st LPC, [k1, p1] twice, k6, [p1, k1] twice, 3-st RPC, p1.

Gayle Bunn's cozy cap provides cool coverage when the mercury dips. It has a chunky center-front cable flanked by smaller cables, a wide ribbed cuff for extra warmth and a big fluffy pompom for show.

KNITTED MEASUREMENTS
■ Head circumference 19½"/49.5cm

MATERIALS
■ 2 2.8oz/80g balls (each approx 110yd/100m) of Patons *SWS* (70% wool/30% soy) in #70117 natural denim
■ One pair each size 8 and 9 (5 and 5.5mm) needles *or size to obtain gauge*
■ Cable needle

GAUGE
17 sts and 21 rows to 4"/10cm over St st using larger needles.
Take time to check gauge.

STITCH GLOSSARY
2-st RT Knit 2nd st on LH needle, then k first st; sl both sts off LH needle.

3-st LPC Sl next 2 sts to cn and hold in *front*, p1, k2 from cn.

3-st RPC Sl next st to cn and hold in *back*, k2, p1 from cn.

3-st LC Sl next 2 sts to cn and hold in *front*, k1, k2 from cn.

3-st RC Sl next st to cn and hold in *back*, k2, k1 from cn.

4-st LC Sl next 2 sts to cn and hold in *front*, k2, k2 from cn.

Row 10 Rep row 6.

Row 11 P2, 3-st LPC, p1, k1, p1, k6, p1, k1, p1, 3-st RPC, p2.

Row 12 Rep row 4.

Row 13 P3, 3-st LPC, k1, p1, 6-st LC, p1, k1, 3-st RPC, p3.

Row 14 Rep row 2.

Row 15 P4, 3-st LPC, p1, k6, p1, 3-st RPC, p4.

Row 16 K5, p12, k5.

Rep rows 1–16 for cable panel B, AT THE SAME TIME, work 6-st LC over center 6 sts every 6 rows.

CAP

Cuff

With smaller needles, cast on 94 sts. Work in cable rib for 3½"/9cm, end on a WS row.

Next (inc) row P across inc 12 sts evenly spaced—106 sts. Change to larger needles.

Note WS of ribbed cuff is RS of crown.

Crown

Row 1 (RS) P2, *2-st RT, p2, work row 1 of cable panel A across next 4 sts, p2*; rep from * to * 3 times more, 2-st RT, work row 1 of cable panel B across next 22 sts; rep from * to * 4 times.

Row 2 *K2, work row 2 of cable panel A across next 4 sts, k2, p2*; rep from * to * 3 times more, work row 2 of cable panel B across next 22 sts, p2; rep from * to * 4 times, k2. Cont to work in pat sts as established until piece measures 7"/18cm from beg, end with a WS row.

Crown shaping

Dec row 1 (RS) P2, *2-st RT, p2tog, work cable panel A across next 4 sts, p2tog*; rep from * to * 3 times more, 2-st RT, work cable panel B across next 22 sts; rep from * to * 4 times—90 sts. Cont to work in pat sts as established for 11 rows.

Dec row 2 (RS) P2, *2-st RT, p1, ssk, k2tog, p1*; rep from * to * 3 times more, 2-st RT, work cable panel B across next 22 sts; rep * to * 4 times—74 sts.

Next row K1, [p2, k1] 7 times, p2, work cable panel B across next 22 sts, [p2, k1] 8 times, p2, k2.

Dec row 3 (RS) P2, [2-st RT, p1] 8 times, 2-st RT, work cable panel B across next 22 sts, [2-st RT, p1] 8 times. Cont to work cable panel B as established, rep last 2 rows once more.

Next row [K1, p2] 8 times, work cable panel B across next 22 sts, [p2, k1] 8 times, p2, k2.

Dec row 4 (RS) P2tog, [k2tog, p1] 8 times, k2tog, work cable panel B across next 22 sts, [k2tog, p1] 8 times—56 sts.

Next row [K1, p1] 8 times, work cable panel B across next 22 sts, [p1, k1] 9 times.

Dec row 5 (RS) *K2tog; rep from * to end—28 sts. Cut yarn leaving a 20"/51cm tail and thread through rem sts. Pull tog tightly and secure end, then sew back seam, rev seam over last 3"/7.5cm for cuff turnback.

POMPOM

Make a 4"/10cm diameter pompom and sew to top of cap.

Cable Panel A
(4 sts)

Cable Panel B
(22 sts)

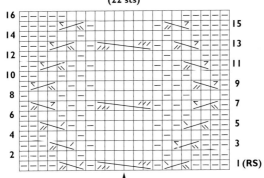

STITCH KEY

☐ K on RS, P on WS

⊟ P on RS, K on WS

(WS) Seed St (RS)

⊠ 2-st RT

3-st RC

3-st LC

3-st RPC

3-st LPC

4-st LC

6-st LC (worked over center 6 sts every 6 rows)

BOMBER HAT

Haute helmet

■■■□▭

Outdoor fun begins with a sporty hat that can take on even the briskest weather. The back flap keeps your neck toasty, while the front flap folds up for style or down when it gets really nippy. It's super-quick to knit using super-bulky yarn and big needles. Designed by Lipp Holmfeld.

KNITTED MEASUREMENTS
■ Head circumference 26"/66cm

MATERIALS
■ 3 3.5oz/100g balls (each approx 45yd/41m) of Blue Sky Alpacas *Bulky Naturals* (50% alpaca/50% wool) in #1004 polar bear (6)
■ One pair size 13 (9mm) needles *or size to obtain gauge*
■ Size 13 (9mm) circular needle, 16"/40cm long *or size to obtain gauge*
■ One set (4) size 13 (9mm) dpn
■ Size I/9 (5.5mm) crochet hook
■ Cable needle
■ Stitch holder
■ Stitch marker

GAUGES
■ 8 sts and 20 rows to 4"/10cm over garter st using size 13 (9mm) needles.
■ 8 sts and 12 rnds to 4"/10cm over cable pat using size 13 (9mm) circular needle.
Take time to check gauges.

STITCH GLOSSARY

2-st LC Sl next st to cn and hold in *front*, k1, k1 from cn.

2-st RC Sl next st to cn and hold in *back*, k1, k1 from cn.

HAT

Ties

With crochet hook, and leaving a 130"/330cm yarn end, ch 26. For first tie, sl st in 2nd ch from hook and in each ch across. Place loop on hook onto a straight needle, then using yarn end and yarn from ball, cast on 29 sts using long-tail cast-on for bottom edge of back flap—30 sts on needle. For second tie, place last st cast on needle onto crochet hook. Ch 26. Sl st in 2nd ch from hook and in each ch across. Place loop on crochet hook back on needle—30 sts on needle.

Back flap

Row 1 (RS) K30.

Row 2 K1, M1, k to last st, M1, k1—32 sts.

Row 3 K32.

Row 4 Rep row 2—34 sts.

Row 5 Knit 34.

Row 6 Rep row 2—36 sts.

Rows 7–12 Knit 36. Place sts on holder.

Front flap

Cast on 18 sts using long-tail cast-on.

Row 1 (RS) K18.

Row 2 K1, M1, k to last st, M1, k1—20 sts.

Row 3 K20.

Row 4 Rep row 2—22 sts.

Row 5 Knit 22.

Row 6 Rep row 2—24 sts.

Rows 7–12 Knit 24.

Joining flaps

With RS facing and circular needle, k 24 sts of front flap, k 18 sts from back flap holder, pm for center back and end of rnds, k 18 sts rem on holder—60 sts. K to marker.

Crown

Rnds 1, 2, 3 and 4 (RS) *P2, k4; rep from * around.

Rnd 5 *P2, 2-st RC, 2-st LC; rep from * around. Rep rnds 1–5 twice more, then work rnds 1–4 once more.

Crown shaping

Note Change to dpn (dividing sts evenly between three needles) when there are too few sts on circular needle.

Dec rnd 1 *P2tog, 2-st RC, 2-st LC; rep from * around—50 sts.

Dec rnd 2 *P1, k2tog, SKP; rep from * around—30 sts.

Next 3 rnds *P1, k2; rep from * around.

Dec rnd 3 *P1, k2tog; rep from * around—20 sts.

Next rnd *P1, k1; rep from * around.

Dec rnd 4 [K2tog] 10 times—10 sts. Cut yarn leaving a 8"/20.5cm tail and thread through rem sts. Pull tog tightly and secure end.

RAPUNZEL HAT

Miss Swiss

Ski slopes have become the fashion venue for wild winter hats, and Gayle Bunn has created one that's fun, warm and quick to knit, too. This novel hat features a chunky cable at center front, playful pompom at the peak and extra-long, tassel-trimmed braids that double as a scarf.

KNITTED MEASUREMENTS

■ Head circumference 22"/56cm

MATERIALS

■ 3 6oz/170g balls (each approx 106yd/97m) of Lion Brand Yarn *Wool-Ease Thick & Quick* (80% acrylic/20% wool) in #122 taupe ⬛

■ One pair size 13 (9mm) needles *or size to obtain gauge*

■ Cable needle

GAUGE

9 sts and 12 rows to 4"/10cm over St st using size 13 (9mm) needles.

Take time to check gauge.

STITCH GLOSSARY

8-st LC Sl next 4 sts to cn and hold in *front*, k4, k4 from cn.

8-st RC Sl next 4 sts to cn and hold in *back*, k4, k4 from cn.

HAT

Cast on 47 sts.

Next row (RS) K1, *p1, k1; rep from * to end. Rep this row once more, inc 3 sts evenly spaced—50 sts.

Beg cable pat

Row 1 (RS) K18, p1, k12, p1, k18.

Row 2 and all WS rows P18, k1, p12, k1, p18.

Row 3 K18, p1, 8-st LC, k4, p1, k18.

Rows 5 and 7 Rep row 1.

Row 9 K18, p1, k4, 8-st RC, p1, k18.

Row 11 Rep row 1.

Row 12 Rep row 2. Rep rows 1–12 until piece measures 6½"/16.5cm from beg, end with a RS row.

Crown shaping

Row 1 (WS) *P3, p2tog; rep from * to end—40 sts.

Rows 2 and 4 Knit.

Row 3 Purl.

Row 5 *P2, p2tog; rep from * to end—30 sts.

Row 6 Knit.

Row 7 [P2tog] 15 times—15 sts. Cut yarn leaving a 20"/51cm tail and thread through rem sts. Pull tog tightly and secure end, then sew back seam.

BRAIDS

Sections (make 6)

Cast on 5 sts. Work in St st until piece measures 48"/122cm from beg, when slightly stretched. Bind off. Allow edges to curl to center. Sew cast-on edges of 3 sections tog. Braid the 3 sections, then sew the bound-off edges tog to secure braid. Make another braid. Beg at top of hat with cast-on end of braid, pin braid to side of hat, positioning it approx 3"/7.5cm from center cable. Sew side edges of braid in place. Sew rem braid on to opposite side of hat.

TASSELS

Wind yarn 12 times around a 4"/10cm piece of cardboard. Make 2 tassels and attach to bound-off ends of braids.

POMPOM

Make a 4½"/11.5cm diameter pompom and sew to top of hat.

Warming Miss Daisy

This dynamic duo is sure to chase away the chill of winter. The hat features a wide cable band, while the neck warmer is ribbed with narrower versions of the same cable. Designed by Melissa Halvorson.

KNITTED MEASUREMENTS

■ Head circumference 20"/51cm
■ Neck warmer 9"/23cm long

MATERIALS

■ 2 3.5oz/100g balls (each approx 175yd/160m) of Louet North America *Gems Worsted* (100% merino wool) in #54 teal (A) **3**
■ 1 ball in #48 aqua (B)
■ One pair size 6 (4mm) needles *or size to obtain gauge*
■ Size 6 (4mm) circular needle, 16"/40cm long
■ One set (4) size 6 (4mm) dpn
■ Cable needle
■ Stitch marker
■ One 1¾"/45mm button
■ 10"/25.5cm length of ¾"/19mm wide snap tape (available at sewing stores)
■ Sewing needle and matching thread

GAUGE

18 sts and 32 rows to 4"/10cm over St st using size 6 (4mm) needles.
Take time to check gauge.

Notes

1 Hat cable band is worked back and forth in rows and the crown is worked in rnds.

2 Neck warmer is made from the top down.

STITCH GLOSSARY

8-st LC Sl next 4 sts to cn and hold in *front*, k4, k4 from cn.

6-st LC Sl next 3 sts to cn and hold in *front*, k3, k3 from cn.

4-st LC Sl next 2 sts to cn and hold in *front*, k2, k2 from cn.

HAT

Cable band

With straight needles and A, cast on 16 sts. Purl next row.

Bag cable pat

Row 1 (RS) K2, p2, 8-st LC, p2, k2.

Row 2 and all WS rows K1, p1, k2, p8, k2, p1, k1.

Rows 3, 5, 7 and 9 K2, p2, k8, p2, k2.

Row 10 Rep row 2. Rep rows 1–10 until piece measures approx 20"/51cm, end with row 4. Bind off. Sew cast-on edge to bound-off edge forming a ring.

Crown

With RS facing, circular needle and B, pick up and k 72 sts along one side edge of cable band, beg and ending at seam. Place marker for end of rnd and sl marker every rnd.

Work in rnds of St st until piece measures 6"/15cm from beg (including cable band), end with a WS row.

Crown shaping

Note Change to dpn when there are too few sts on circular needle.

Rnd 1 (RS) *K7, k2tog; rep from * around—64 sts.

Rnd 2 *K6, k2tog; rep from * around—56 sts.

Rnd 3 *K5, k2tog; rep from * around—48 sts

Rnd 4 *K4, k2tog; rep from * around—40 sts.

Rnd 5 *K3, k2tog; rep from * around—32 sts.

Rnd 6 *K2, k2tog; rep from * around—24 sts.

Rnd 7 *K1, k2tog; rep from * around—16 sts.

Rnd 8 [K2tog] 8 times—8 sts. Cut yarn leaving a 6"/15.5cm tail and thread through rem sts. Pull tog tightly and secure end.

FINISHING

Position button on top of cable band seam; sew in place.

NECK WARMER

Beg at top edge, with straight needles and A, cast on 98 sts. Purl next row.

Beg cable pat 1

Rows 1 and 3 (RS) K1, p1, k4, *p2, k4; rep from * to last 2 sts, end p1, k1.

Row 2 and all WS rows K2, *p4, k2; rep from * to end.

Row 5 K1, p1, 4-st LC, *p2, 4-st LC; rep from * to last 2 sts, end p1, k1.

Row 6 Rep row 2.

Rows 7–12 Rep rows 1–6.

Rows 13–18 Rep rows 1 and 2 3 times.

Row (dec) 19 K1, p1, *sl next 2 sts to cn and hold in *front*, k2tog, SKP from cn, p2; rep from * end last rep p1, k1 (instead of p2)—66 sts.

Beg rib pat

Row 1 (WS) K2, *p2, k2; rep from * to end.

Row 2 K1, p1, k2, *p2, k2; from * to last 2 sts, end p1, k1. Rep rows 1 and 2 until piece measures 5½"/14cm from beg, end with a WS row.

Beg cable pat 2

Row (inc) 1 (RS) K1, p1, *place horizontal strand between last st and next st on cn, then sl next st on cn, hold in *front*, M1, k in front and back of next st, sl sts on cn back to LH needle, k1, k in front and back of next st, p2; rep from * end last rep p1, k1 instead of p2)—130 sts.

Row 2 and all WS rows K2, *p6, k2; rep from * to end.

Rows 3, 5 and 7 K1, p1, k6, *p2, k6; rep from * to last 2 sts, end p1, k1.

Row 9 K1, p1, 6-st LC, *p2, 6-st LC; rep from * to last 2 sts, end p1, k1.

Row 11 Rep row 3.

Row 12 Rep row 2. Rep rows 3–12 once more, then rows 3–8 once. Bind off all sts knitwise.

Snap plackets

With RS facing and B, pick up and k32 sts evenly spaced along right front edge. Beg with a p row, cont in St st for 6 rows. Bind off loosely knitwise. Rep on left front edge. Unsnap the snap tape. For right snap placket, fold short edges of top side of snap tape ½"/1.3cm to WS; press. Pin snap tape to WS of placket. Whipstitch around entire edge of snap tape using sewing thread. For left snap placket, fold short edges of bottom side of snap tape ½"/1.3cm to WS; press. Pin snap tape to RS of placket. Whipstitch around entire edge of snap tape using sewing thread.

RESOURCES

*Write to the yarn
companies listed below for
purchasing and mail-order
information.*

Berroco, Inc.
P. O. Box 367
14 Elmdale Road
Uxbridge, MA 01569
www.berroco.com

Blue Sky Alpacas
P. O. Box 88
Cedar MN 55011
www.blueskyalpacas.com

Classic Elite Yarns
122 Western Avenue
Lowell, MA 01851
www.classiceliteyarns.com

Coats & Clark
3430 Toringdon Way,
Suite 301
Charlotte, NC 28277
www.coatsandclark.com

Colinette
distributed by
Unique Kolours
www.colinette.com

Dale of Norway
4750 Shelburne Road
Shelburne, VT 05482
www.dale.no

Filatura Di Crosa
distributed by
Tahki•Stacy Charles, Inc.

KFI
P.O. Box 336
315 Bayview Avenue
Amityville, New York 11701
www.knittingfever.com

Lion Brand Yarn
34 West 15th Street
New York, NY 10011
www.lionbrand.com

Lorna's Laces
4229 North Honore Street
Chicago, IL 60613
www.lornaslaces.net

Louet North America
808 Commerce Park Drive
Ogdensburg, NY 13669

Mission Falls
156 Lawrence Paquette
Champlain, NY 12919
www.missionfalls.com

Moda Dea
distributed by
Coats & Clark
www.modeadea.com

Nashua Handknits
distributed by
Westminster Fibers, Inc.

RYC
distributed by
Westminster Fibers, Inc.

Sublime
distributed by
KFI

Tahki•Stacy Charles, Inc.
70-30 80th Street
Building #36
Ridgewood, NY 11385
www.tahkistacycharles.com

Trendsetter Yarns
16745 Saticoy Street #101
Van Nuys, CA 91406
www.trendsetter.com

Unique Kolours
28 N. Bacton Road
Malvern, PA 19355
www.uniquekolours.com

Westminster Fibers
165 Ledge Street
Nashua, NH 03060
www.westminsterfibers.com

*Write to U.S. resources
for mail-order availability
of yarns not listed.*

Koigu Wool Designs
Box 158
563295 Glenelg Holland
   Townline
Chatsworth, Ontario
Canada N0H1G0
www.koigu.com

Louet North America
R.R. 4
Prescott, Ontario
Canada K0E 1T0
www.louet.com

Mission Falls
5333 Casgrain #1204
Montreal, QC
Canada H2T 1X3
www.missionfalls.com

Patons
320 Livingstone Avenue
   South
Listowel, Ontario
Canada N4W 3H3
www.patonsyarns.com

CABLES **ON THE GO!**

Editorial Director
ELAINE SILVERSTEIN

Book Division Manager
ERICA SMITH

Executive Editor
CARLA S. SCOTT

Art Director
DIANE LAMPHRON

Associate Art Director
SHEENA T. PAUL

Yarn Editor
TANIS GRAY

Instructions Editors
PAT HARSTE
JEANNIE CHIN

Photography
JACK DEUTSCH STUDIO

Copy Editor
KRISTINA SIGLER

Vice President, Publisher
TRISHA MALCOLM

Production Manager
DAVID JOINNIDES

Creative Director
JOE VIOR

President
ART JOINNIDES

LOOK FOR THESE OTHER TITLES IN *ON THE GO!* SERIES...